Investing Psychology
Secrets

LOUISE BEDFORD

Bestselling author of *Charting Secrets* and *Trading Secrets*

Investing
Psychology
Secrets

SURE-FIRE, **DATA-DRIVEN STRATEGIES**
TO SUPERCHARGE YOUR TRADING RESULTS

WILEY

First published in 2024 by John Wiley & Sons Australia, Ltd
Level 4, 600 Bourke St, Melbourne, Victoria 3000, Australia

Typeset in Utopia Std 10.5 pt/14.5pt

© Trading Secrets Pty Ltd 2024

The moral rights of the author have been asserted

ISBN: 978-1-394-26400-1

 A catalogue record for this
book is available from the
National Library of Australia

Cover design by Wiley
Cover image: © Mariia/Adobe Stock
Internal key icon: © Tartila/Adobe Stock
Printed and bound by CPI Group (UK) Ltd, Croydon, CR0 4YY

Disclaimer

C9781394264001_130524

Contents

PROLOGUE
Let's kick off

I opened my mouth to answer my daughter's question… and no sound came out.

Nothing at all… not even a squeak.

I'd had trouble with my voice for the past decade, but never to this extent. Something had shifted, deep inside my throat. A strange openness. An inability to connect. I could barely even swallow.

It was December 15th, 2019. I was on a holiday with my youngest child, Ash. She was 12.

Little did I imagine this would be my new reality.

I'd caught a virus that triggered a cascade of pain, and an inability to make any noise whatsoever for nine months. Related to a problem I'd had in my twenties (when I lost the ability to move my arms for around three years), it felt strangely familiar… and terrifying.

I was alone in my silent world while the pandemic surged, unable to talk with my family or friends, or even do a Zoom call. I'd never felt so isolated. Inwardly I was screaming from the injustice of it. Raging silently, and wondering whether this would be my reality forever.

Despite intensive speech therapy and a vast array of painful exercises designed to get sound flowing again, it would be two years before I could speak my first hoarse and scratchy sentence.

It's a strange thing to have your body turn against you and not to know whether you'll be able to return to full strength. It's demoralising and humiliating. Waves of grief overwhelmed me. The horror of my situation felt suffocating. Unable to chat with friends, or even talk over the dinner table with my children and husband, I withdrew.

It was subtle at first. But soon I found myself shunning everyone because I felt so damned vulnerable. I became the object of other people's jokes as so-called friends said, 'I'll bet your husband is loving this!' I was appalled by the tactlessness. Their words cut into my already fragile heart.

Then it dawned on me. *This* was a mind game. It was a psychological challenge designed to test whether I was resilient enough to make it through.

Because, by heck, the universe will screw with you. It will treat your plans like a game of Jenga. But how you respond… what you do with your hurts, your discomforts and your disappointments… this is what's really important.

I turned to the lessons the markets had provided me. I sensed that within them were the seeds of my recovery.

Thank goodness I had investing as a back-up plan. Having traded for over 30 years, I had an edge in the markets, which meant I didn't lose my job because I was *already* a full-time investor.

I really don't know what would have become of me if I had been pursuing a regular career when I lost my voice, because 99 per cent of jobs expect you to be able to talk.

I hung onto the words of the Roman poet Ovid: 'Someday this pain will be useful to you.' They were my life raft. I repeated them in my mind like a mantra.

I threw myself into research. What mind hacks could I find to improve my situation? What could help me — both to advance my recovery and to give my investing a boost?

Investing Psychology Secrets is the culmination of that research. In this book I combine my personal experiences as an investor and trader for more than 30 years with data-driven, science-backed, high-performance methods to propel your results to the next level.

Over the past four years I've regained my ability to speak more or less reliably. I still experience setbacks, but I have been able to move through them. And even though I still need regular speech therapy to maintain my voice, I'm much better than I was in those initial months when I was terrified I might never speak again.

Sure, life may let you down. You might experience illness, retrenchment or disappointment.

Today you may suffer fools, face hostility or have to deal with people who despise everything you value in life. Maybe you aren't cared for in a way that makes your soul sing. It may seem like the markets are out to get you and you'll never be the consistent performer you want to be.

The question is, what are you going to do about it?

Listen to that voice. The one telling you that you deserve more.

Let no one keep you from improving your financial future:

Not the mother who wants you to fulfil her ambitions vicariously.

Not the father who expects you to follow the old rules for building wealth.

Not the domineering teacher who can't see you're about to spread your wings.

Not the employer who frustrates you with their unreasonable demands.

Not the voice that whispers in your ear at 3 am, 'You're not good enough.'

Let *nothing* dissuade you.

Your investor's life awaits. You're about to unlock the mindset secrets you'll need to excel in the markets. And I'll be with you every step of the way, drawing on high-performance research to soothe your frazzled mind. The lessons I'll share with you are relevant no matter what time frame you trade in, what pocket of the financial markets you focus on. You'll benefit whether you consider yourself a trader or an investor.

What I'm about to share with you is nothing short of revolutionary. It is your key to developing mental toughness so you can trade consistently in the markets and overcome that nagging self-doubt.

The keys to success

In this book I'll build on many of the ideas I explore on my *Talking Trading* podcast (www.talkingtrading.com.au). I'll show you specific techniques you can use to change the way you look at the markets and yourself. The way to excel in the markets is to detach yourself from your results, and the way to do this is to develop your psychological fitness.

Investing Psychology Secrets is a bench press for your mind. Put in a little consistent effort now, and you'll stretch, develop and grow. You're about to learn why some investors beat the markets ... and why most don't.

There are the six golden keys to psychological fitness, and we'll work through each of them together:

Key 1: Success habits. Build winning routines for exceptional investing and trading.

Key 2: Emotional mastery. Keep your cool and flourish.

Key 3: Money mindset. Know yourself to boost your profits.

Key 4: Recharge and renew. Stay energised for optimal performance.

Key 5: Motivation. Use inspiration to drive your results forward.

Key 6: Prime your mind for success. Stories and exercises to reprogram your subconscious.

Read this book starting from the beginning if you'd like. If you're after a quick two-minute boost, though, I suggest you choose one of the stories and exercises from Key 6 to give you the lift you need. Many investors choose to dip into that key for a bedtime story, so their minds are primed for the next day's market action.

At the end of each chapter, I list the key concepts for you as a way of reinforcing the core lessons. When you want a quick refresher, you can turn to those sections for a reminder of the main skills to focus on.

Yes, you may feel a bit vulnerable while reading this book. It may even make you feel a bit queasy when you realise how much money you've left on the table because of your own limitations. But now is the time you put your foot down and get out of your own freaking way to scoop up the rewards the financial markets have to offer.

Trading vs investing

Everything I'm about to relay applies whether you identify as a trader or an investor.

In Australia and some other regions, investors generally have different tax advantages compared to traders. Investors also may choose longer term instruments such as ETFs (exchange traded funds), shares and managed funds, whereas traders may be more attracted to using CFDs (contracts for difference) and derivatives, profiting from sideways movement and downtrends, rather than just uptrends. Many investors adopt a 'buy and hold' strategy.

Some may not even use a trading plan. (Yikes! Perish the thought!) A trading plan is needed by all traders *and* investors to guide how they interact with the market. It helps you decide how to get into positions, how to get out and how much money to put into each position.

To improve your performance, document your trading plan and include all possible scenarios. A written plan reduces the burden on your working memory (your brain's short-term information storage), especially in high-pressure situations. If you'd like my free trading plan template, go to www.tradinggame.com.au

and register your details, and I'll email it to you straight away. Following a predetermined plan reduces stress and increases the likelihood of consistent decision making, which will help you achieve success.

Even if you think of yourself as an investor, I urge you to consider carefully and *document* your entry, exit and position sizing. It's one of the keys to success. Although I'll be focusing on investing in the financial markets, even if you're investing in another asset class, such as property, collectables or a business, these mindset tricks are equally relevant.

Show a bit of mental flexibility here. You might think of yourself as a trader rather than an investor — or vice versa. But I use these terms interchangeably throughout the book. The lessons I convey can be applied regardless of your time horizon or how you define your financial activities.

Are you a survivor?

Ever watched the TV show *Survivor*? The goal is to outwit, outlast and outplay your opponents (while being starved, sunburned and semi-tortured in the cause of 'entertainment'). Investing is a bit like that, except the person you're competing against is yourself. You have to outwit, outlast and outplay yourself, performing at the top of your game. That's where the prize lies.

Being a great investor is a gradual, incremental by-product of this activity, not an outcome. It is the fruit of the seed you diligently and lovingly planted. People who do well in the markets exhibit a unique combination of strength, endurance and resilience. These qualities don't come naturally to most of us, but they are exactly what you'll gain by reading this book.

Do you want to discover what it means to be a psychologically fit market dynamo? Join me on this journey and you'll develop your psychological flexibility so you're equipped to handle everything the markets throw at you. There'll be triumphs, struggles, vexation and breakthroughs. You'll learn how to keep your money firmly in your account, how to grow it consistently, and how to stop giving away your hard-earned gains due to rookie mistakes.

I'll give you the tools you need to become a truly consistent performer. Let's start by looking at the success habits required for you to build exceptional investing and trading skills ...

KEY 1

Success habits

*Build winning routines
for exceptional investing
and trading*

Imagine putting your investing on autopilot. You don't have to think deeply about every decision. You can really concentrate on the aspects of your life that are more personally meaningful. You'll achieve exceptional results without any extra effort. And if you can work out a way to prevent bad habits from taking hold, it will free up your life, right?

It's essential to develop habits that permit you to devote less conscious time to the repetitive aspects of your life. Habits let you free up your working memory, allowing you to think more deeply about things that really matter. Because if every minor decision has to be painstakingly thought through, you'll soon drain your battery, and be more likely to make mistakes.

Behavioural finance expert Brett Steenbarger is spot on when he says, 'The right trading behaviours start as rules and evolve into habits.'

We are the sum of the habits we create. Around half of our everyday behaviours are performed automatically, with little forethought. However, you need to develop conscious awareness of these behaviours. Any habits formed should feed into the goal of developing exceptional trading skills, and not be the equivalent of acting mindlessly.

Key reasons to develop good habits

There are three reasons why you should make the effort to develop good habits:

1. Good habits minimise decision fatigue

If you don't develop effective trading habits, decision fatigue can set in. Past a certain threshold, each extra decision you make taxes your working memory, and your ability to make additional decisions is reduced.

Sure, the first few decisions you make when you're feeling fresh might be carefully considered, but as the day continues, each new decision will wear down your working memory, and your ability to make additional decisions will suffer.

Think of it like a game of chess. You start with a lot of pieces and a lot of moves to make. But as the game progresses, you lose some pieces and your options become more limited. So it's important to practise your early moves in order for them to become habitual. That way you can save your energy for more important decisions later on.

2. Good habits help ensure you always keep learning

Freeing up your working memory allows more room for deep thought. Effective trading requires a combination of following good routines and course corrections when you've made sub-optimal decisions. If you're always fighting mini-fires, you just won't have time to think deeply about your next strategic move.

3. Good habits give you a confidence boost

When you're disciplined and doing what it takes, you feel like a financial market superstar. Your confidence grows when you stick to your routines and make well-informed decisions.

Success hinges on more than just routine actions. It demands conscious engagement, deliberate choices and a deep understanding of your own behaviour. Every habit you form should be intricately woven into the fabric of your trading goals, fuelling your journey towards mastery.

That's where we're starting our journey towards developing psychological fitness. You'll learn how to develop habits with ease, to drop habits that aren't contributing to your goals, and to avoid habits that could deplete your bank account.

It's time to get rolling…

CHAPTER 1

Why is psychological fitness essential?

Why is developing your mindset so important? Surely it's the 'system' you use that determines your success? Well, think again. This is exactly why you should work as hard on your mindset as you do on your trading plan.

I'm about to propose something controversial here: *All success starts in the mind.* Bank accounts are built one step behind the level of your mindset. The sooner you can accept this, the better. When you first dive into trading, you might think success depends solely on the system you use. But let me tell you, it's only after you've faced a few setbacks that you realise the real game-changer is your mindset. You've got to be prepared to dive deep into your tub of emotional goo to come out the other side as an exceptional trader.

Investors start their journey fuelled by excitement about the boundless potential of the markets. The initial enthusiasm sweeping over you can lead to optimism bias, which causes you to overestimate your likelihood of success. It becomes all too easy to overlook or downplay any potential negative consequences.

Most people think the future will be easier, brighter, better. They feel they'll have more time, resources, abilities. Sadly, though, things don't usually turn out as well as we anticipate.

Researcher Sharot found, 'When it comes to predicting what will happen to us tomorrow, next week, or fifty years from now, we overestimate the likelihood of positive events, and underestimate the likelihood of negative events.' For example, we underrate our chances of divorce, being in an accident or suffering from a serious illness, while also expecting to live longer than expected, overestimating job success or believing our children will be prodigies. This tendency translates directly into the financial markets, especially when we're starting out.

Traders swing between extremes. If they're not overly optimistic, they are in despair about the markets and their own abilities. Consumed by thoughts of destitution, homelessness and uncertainty, they envision a bleak future. I like to think of this as *awfulising*. Psychologists use the term *catastrophising*. Either way, you surround everyday events in your life with drama to feel the adrenaline surge through your body. Researchers Sullivan et al. define catastrophising as 'an exaggerated negative "mental set" brought to bear during painful experiences'. More simply, it's the tendency to imagine the worst.

As a trader, however, you can't afford to awfulise. There are consequences. Why? Because you may just awfulise a totally 'normal' situation and freak yourself out. If you constantly surround your trading with drama, you might also put some of the people who care about you offside. They'll seek to protect you, instead of being your cheerleader.

Drop awfulising now!

The price of awfulising is just too high. To avoid it, ask yourself three questions about the 'calamity' you're facing:

1. 'Is it true?'

2. 'What evidence is there for this?'

3. 'Is it useful?'

If the way you're thinking is not true, or if the evidence for it is scanty and it's not a useful way of thinking, you need to drop that line of thought.

From time to time the market can seem like it's attacking us personally. If you've ever popped money into a position and immediately the damned thing goes against your wishes, I can tell you, it's hard not to take it personally. But it's not just when you're making a loss that you have to think about your own psychology. It's also when things go well.

Top-notch investing is not just about mastering technical skills. You also need to train your mind to handle the ups and downs of the trading world. This means developing coping strategies, managing your emotions and staying in control. It's essential to work on building your self-esteem and staying optimistic, while still being realistic about your abilities. Don't worry if this doesn't come naturally to you — most traders need to work on these areas to develop psychological fitness.

Psychological fitness

Psychological fitness means having the ability to grow and bounce back from significant challenges. And, just like physical fitness, it's something you can actively work on and control through training.

When you accept that anything can happen in the markets but it's your mission to assess probabilities, you're on the right track. Only take trades when the evidence indicates that the trend you're backing will continue. If you truly believe this, then you won't block, deny or attack anything the market is offering. You'll respond with clinical detachment, basing your decisions on the weight of evidence.

To achieve this goal, you must train your mindset in various ways. You need to develop coping strategies, manage your emotions and maintain self-control. For most traders, this level of self-awareness isn't automatic.

Five reasons to improve your psychological fitness

Here are five reasons you should prioritise improving your psychological fitness. It will help you:

- **develop detachment.** To make objective decisions and avoid investing emotionally, you need to develop detachment towards your results. You've made a 'good trade' if you've followed your trading plan to the letter (regardless of the profit or loss you make). When you are at peace with any outcome of your trading, you'll be free to trade with precision.

- **open up to new possibilities.** Improving your psychological fitness sparks your curiosity and eagerness to explore new areas. You become more adventurous and develop a genuine thirst for knowledge.

- **embrace resilience.** Psychological fitness strengthens your resilience, making you less likely to give up and more inclined to persevere. You become better equipped to face challenges head-on, bounce back from setbacks, invest more effort and find inspiration in the achievements of others.

- **stay grounded.** Working on your psychological fitness keeps you humble, preventing both overconfidence and self-doubt from clouding your judgement. Interestingly, studies have shown that overly confident traders tend to earn lower profits in their trades.

- **learn from your mistakes.** By improving your psychological fitness, you develop the ability to learn from past mistakes. This ensures that you'll stay in the markets long enough to make necessary course corrections.

Emotional discipline may be even more important than having a good system. Writing in his very popular book *The New Market Wizards*, Jack Schwager puts it this way:

> *If there is a single theme that keeps recurring in this volume, as it did in* Market Wizards, *it is that psychology is critical to success at trading. In order to achieve success in life, you must have the right mental attitude.*

If trading (or any other endeavour) is a source of anxiety, fear, frustration, depression, or anger, something is wrong — even if you are successful in the conventional sense, and especially if you're not.

You have to enjoy trading, because if trading is a source of negative emotions, you have probably already lost the game, even if you make money.

Sadly, sometimes *you* can be your own worst enemy. Especially when the market seems to turn against you, it can be hard to decide to pick up the pieces and give trading another shot.

The late psychologist and author, Dr Harry Stanton, was my friend and co-author of our book *Let the Trade Wins Flow*. Let me tell you how I got to know him … and eventually had the honour of writing a book with him on trading psychology.

Harry is the sole reason I decided to study psychology at university. Frankly, he turned my life around when, as a 15-year-old, I was heading towards a very bad place. My darling sister, Valerie, gave me his book, *The Plus Factor*. I still have the original copy, printed in 1979, on my bookshelf. This book touched my heart. More importantly, it made me realise that my future was in *my* hands.

His words comforted me and made me feel less alone. They spoke to me. After the first three pages, I knew I had found my calling. I was determined to study psychology at university so I could gain insights into how people's minds worked … and how *my* mind worked. Years later Harry and I became friends. He shared with me his views about the markets and candle charts, and our friendship deepened.

Harry summed up beautifully my tendency to become ecstatic one minute and to plunge into the depths of despair the next. As a trader, especially when you're starting out, you'll swing from excessive optimism to abject despair like a little pendulum wrecking ball. The key to high performance, Harry told me, was to be less emotionally volatile, develop objectivity and always take a pause before making big decisions.

Emotional Distance

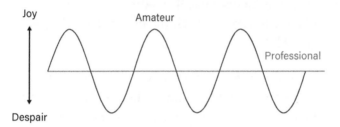

It's so easy to climb on board a joy/despair roller-coaster, but in reality you'll make your best decisions when you adopt a more level-headed approach. When you feel like your belly is doing flip-flops because of this joy/despair cycle, personal mantras can help.

As a beginner, I cried about every loss I made. Not just one of those pretty soap opera weeps with tears rolling delicately down my face. I'm talking about a howling, red-faced blotchy mess. Yet every profit had me dancing around the house, singing 'I wanna be a billionaire' at the top of my lungs.

It took me a very long time to calm the heck down.

Common biases

We're subject to a bunch of biases that can foul up our thinking and impact our investing results. Here are some of the biases that can affect you:

- **Confirmation bias:** We all hear what we want to hear, and investors tend to listen only to the news that tells them they're right.

- **Overconfidence bias:** If you think you're the guru of the financial markets, you might take risks you shouldn't.

- **Loss aversion:** No one likes losing money. But many people hate it so much they hold onto losing investments forever, hoping they'll magically turn into winners.

- **Herding behaviour:** Investors can blindly follow the crowd, even when it's not the smartest move.

- **Anchoring bias:** Imagine you bought a stock at $50. Now it's at $30, but you're convinced it'll go back to $50. Anchoring bias makes you hang on, even if your hunch is unlikely.

- **Recency bias:** Recent events have a big impact on our decisions. If the market's been great lately, we may imagine it'll stay that way forever.

- **Availability bias:** We're often influenced by what's in front of us. If the news is screaming about a particular company, we might jump in without thinking.

- **Hindsight bias:** Ever said, 'I knew that would happen!' after the event? That's hindsight bias making us feel smarter than we really are.

- **Endowment effect:** We tend to think our stuff is more valuable just because it's ours. Same goes for stocks we own — we may hang on when we should let go.

- **Disposition effect:** Selling winners too early and holding on to losers — that's the disposition effect in action.

Unless we are aware of these effects and work out ways around them in advance, we can struggle in the markets. After I learned about these biases, I began to recognise many of them in my own behaviour. They were part of the puzzle, but not the complete answer.

Metacognition

Only humans have the special ability to think about their own thinking. It's called 'metacognition'. You can totally use this ability to level up your life, boost your performance and bounce back from tough life events.

The more you fine-tune your skills by examining your own behaviour and motivations, the less your unconscious mind can wreak havoc on your trading outcomes. It's quite possible two people can use the same trading system but end up with different results. It all boils down to how they think about money, the markets and themselves.

Developing the right mindset is an absolute game-changer, especially when it comes to gaining an edge in the markets. By making consistent and calculated decisions, rather than being buffeted by their emotions, these traders achieve more regular positive results.

However, all of this can take some time and effort.

The research strongly suggests that if you can stay in the arena for longer, you're more likely to be successful. Developing your psychological fitness can help you become resilient, so you're more likely to give yourself time to develop and grow as a trader.

Fixed vs growth mindset

In *Mindset: The New Psychology of Success*, Carol Dweck unveils a fascinating divergence in how people approach the world. People have either a fixed mindset or a growth mindset.

I caught up with a trader the other day and he said, 'Well, if I haven't made it by now as a trader, I'll never make it.' This is a sign of a fixed mindset. Traders with a fixed mindset tend to think they have reached their upper limit of endeavour and can never grow further.

Study after study has shown that those with a fixed mindset are more likely to give up, or even cheat on tests. Why do they cheat? Well, they feel that if the questions are difficult, a bad test result will threaten their self-identity as being 'clever', and they'll fight to maintain this image of themselves. They'll quit for the same reason. It's easier to quit than to persevere in a field that's challenging.

A fixed mindset person:

- tends to shy away from challenges in just about every area of their lives

- is quick to quit when obstacles pop up

- thinks putting effort into tasks is pointless so looks for short cuts

- would rather ignore helpful criticism than use it to make positive changes

- is intimidated or threatened by the success of others.

What about those with a growth mindset? Well, these people love learning new things. They're not tied to the outcome, so they continue to grow and achieve. They adore the process.

The growth mindset person:

- embraces challenges

- perseveres in spite of setbacks

- knows achieving goals takes effort and is willing to put in the work

- listens and learns from criticism

- finds the success of others inspirational.

When you have a growth mindset, you believe you can gain the knowledge and skills necessary to succeed, which makes every challenge a learning opportunity.

If there's one goal every trader should share, it's to develop consistency, even though it's a difficult skill to learn. Consistency is more likely if you develop a growth mindset, so you can learn from your mistakes and continue investing.

Key concepts

- If you keep thinking the same old way you always have, don't be surprised when you keep getting the same old results.

- Beware of optimism bias, which causes you to overestimate your likelihood of success.

- Minimise your awfulising, where you surround yourself with drama and exaggerate negative impacts on your life.

- Professionals in the markets aim to maintain emotional stability rather than swinging between joy and despair.

- Your target is to develop psychological fitness and a growth mindset. You're more likely to be open to new possibilities, resilient and humble, and to learn from your mistakes.

Effective habits are at the core of consistent returns. But what if you're not really sure how to initiate your new habit? And once you've developed a habit, how do you maintain it so your actions can run on autopilot, freeing your mind to think about higher-level strategies? You'll find out in the next chapter ...

CHAPTER 2

Start, damn it ... start

This is how to initiate new habits so you can become an exceptional trader. Procrastination will be consigned to the past once you've read this chapter.

Tim Pychyl, author of *Solving the Procrastination Puzzle*, defines a number of task characteristics that make you more likely to procrastinate.

Repellent tasks tend to be:

- boring

- frustrating

- difficult

- lacking in personal meaning and intrinsic rewards

- ambiguous (you don't know how to do them).

Studies show that when we procrastinate, we get an instant kick of endorphins, but then, over time, we actually feel more stressed than we would be if we hadn't procrastinated. People who habitually procrastinate have more stress-related health problems. And people who beat themselves up because they've procrastinated are more likely to experience depression.

Clearly, procrastination is something you need to overcome to be a successful trader. And the simplest way to overcome procrastination is to adopt habits that become a part of your everyday life.

Which habits?

What habits do you personally need to adopt to improve your investing practice? Make a list so you know exactly what you're aiming for. Here are some ideas:

- Set a time/day to review your charts and analyse the markets.

- Analyse your trading plan results at least every six months.

- Revise your trading plan annually.

- Set a stop loss every time you place a trade. A stop loss is an order which closes an open position at a predetermined price level.

- Enter your trade details in your portfolio manager promptly.

- Develop and use a consistent method for position sizing your trades.

- Keep up to date with the paperwork required for tax time.

- Track your results regularly with a trading friend/mentor.

- Keep in touch with an investing community so you can associate with like-minded people.

- Keep running your scans so you don't get out of practice (even if there are no opportunities to trade because you're fully invested).

- Keep a journal to record what you did well and what you should do differently.

- If you have a spouse, schedule a 'boardroom meeting' to update them on essential developments.

- Set aside some time to examine the trades you *don't* take. Did any of them skyrocket, and if so, can you work out why? Are there any lessons here?

- Review the trades where you were stopped out. Was your stop in the right place, or do you need to rejig your methods for future trades?

It can feel a bit daunting, can't it? Yet often the first step is the hardest.

When it comes to long-term behaviour change, you frequently hear about the importance of *maintenance* — the stage where habits are solidified and effortlessly integrated into our lives. But what about the crucial *initiation* phase that precedes it? Many people have a clear vision of the behaviour they want to adopt and the goal they want to achieve, but they procrastinate on taking the first step.

Or, if you've needed to take a break from the markets, re-establishing your previous trading habits can feel just as daunting. So this chapter is for you too.

We're all dopamine addicts. We love that little neurological squirt of dopamine, the feel-good hormone, when we do something 'right'. Dopamine reinforces the habit and makes it more likely we'll repeat that behaviour. However, the first step to generating a dopamine thrill is *initiating* action.

Let's get going

The other day I got a phone call from my old friend Roy. You'd love Roy. He's a corporate guy, wise beyond belief and a true professional. Roy was originally my inspiration for getting involved in the sharemarket when I was 20 years old. He knows everything about trading, and about making money. Now, all of that would be impressive, except for the fact Roy still hasn't placed his first trade!

Yes, that's right. For one reason or another, Roy just hasn't made the leap of faith it takes to actually buy his first share. Now that's extreme procrastination! He should be inducted into the Procrastinators Hall of Fame! Multiple decades of faffing around, with no results to show for all his vast reserves of intellect.

Don't end up like Roy—forever looking to learn, but never brave enough to jump in. The world is full of educated derelicts, always on the sidelines, never experiencing the rush of a profitable trade and the buzz of self-discovery. There's nothing like that moment of realisation when you discover you're the type of trader who can make money no matter what the market is doing. Sure, initiating change can be challenging. It's natural to feel resistance, fear or uncertainty. But by understanding the psychology behind behaviour change, you can navigate around these obstacles and pave the way to transformation.

Science-backed techniques for habit formation

There are three little-known, sure-fire methods you can use to develop enduring habits:

1. Fresh start psychology

The psychological phenomenon called the *fresh start effect* can significantly increase your chances of success when embracing life changes.

> *You attach a landmark or milestone as a symbolic pin on the map of your reality. This is the Fresh Start Effect. It acts as a mental accounting period, allowing you to leave behind mistakes of the past and start again with enthusiasm.*

The feeling you're beginning again is most commonly associated with the start of a new year, but it can be triggered at any time. Starting a new job, moving to a different city, celebrating a birthday, even welcoming a new month ... each can serve as a fresh start, offering an opportunity to redefine your investing habits and set yourself on a path to success.

Researchers have discovered an intriguing link between the fresh start effect and an individual's mindset. It seems that the extent to which you can harness this psychological phenomenon for your own benefit depends on whether you possess a growth mindset or a fixed mindset. Those with the shrewdest financial minds also have stronger 'fresh start mindsets' and tend to exhibit traits such as a higher capacity for personal change, optimism and an internal locus of control.

Chris Tate, author of *The Art of Trading,* suggests, 'Too often traders look outwards for what is essentially an internal problem. The ability to create a calm, still mind solves a myriad of trading problems.'

Traders with an external locus of control:

- experience frequent self-doubt

- blame their broker, spouse or 'experts' when they make a loss

- have trouble learning from past experience because they do not take responsibility

- try to prove they are 'right' rather than minimising their losses when a trade turns against them

- react emotionally.

Traders with an internal locus of control:

- usually have a realistic understanding of their own abilities

- know they are completely responsible for their own actions

- do not rely predominantly on 'expert advice', such as from a broker or tip sheets

- know they cannot control the markets, only themselves

- react objectively.

When I was broke, I used to spout drivel about why it wasn't my fault. One day I just stopped, cold turkey. Things turned around pretty quickly after that. Coincidence? I think not. Making excuses is a malignant force in your life. You will repel people if you're a whinger. It's also a sign you're deluded about your life, and a sad demonstration of your personal lack of integrity. If you continue to blame circumstances, you'll rob yourself of the chance to face reality and make the adjustments to your life that will underpin your future success.

Hold yourself accountable. Stop accepting your own nonsense. Demand a higher standard from yourself.

The implications of this are profound, especially when it comes to breaking habits. Take smoking, for example. While most people agree it's a habit worth breaking, the chances of successfully quitting and avoiding a relapse can be tied to major life events that trigger fresh starts. Researchers McDermott, Dobson and Russell report, 'Life changes such as marriage and actual or contemplated pregnancy provide opportunities for targeted interventions to help women quit smoking and not relapse after having a baby.'

You can apply this powerful technique in your own investing journey. Consider linking your new habit to a distinct 'before and after' snapshot of your life. For instance, you might say, 'Before I read Louise's book, I struggled to stick to my stop-loss orders. Now I make a point of always following a stop-loss order when I trade!'

Identify meaningful milestones in your life and use them as anchors to initiate positive change in your trading habits. With each new beginning, you have the chance to recalibrate, learn from past experiences and approach the markets with renewed commitment.

2. Your future self

Research suggests that strong habits will dominate, even if you are motivated to achieve an entirely different goal.

Picture this: You want to be a skilled trader, but your habit of partying every weekend undermines your time for market analysis. This habit will dominate unless you implement the following very effective strategy.

Imagine your future self — a year from now — having mastered trading skills and filled crucial knowledge gaps. You'll be magnetically drawn to this new image of yourself if you visualise it in enough detail. I guarantee it will boost your chances of success.

We imagine we'll be the same person tomorrow as we are today. We think, 'I am who I am.' We cling to our identity. Psychologists call this identity foreclosure.

Yet over time, we change, we grow and we alter our views.

Have you ever had a bit of a chuckle when you've read something you wrote when you were a teenager? That's an example of how our personality and identity change over time. But the funny thing is, we underestimate how much we are likely to change in the future.

We forget how resilient we are in the face of change. We get scared about taking on new challenges because so many of us are change-averse. We think we'll never adjust.

Give yourself some credit. You have adapted and grown so much over your life. You will do the same in the future.

Think about the trader you want to become and let that 'future you' draw you forward. Research suggests the more goal driven you become, the easier it will be to create habits that will shape your future view. The clearer your goals, the more your daily actions align with your aspirations. Be crystal clear and watch your behaviour pave the way to success. For example, many traders have the goal of becoming a full-time trader. In chapter 43 you'll find a checklist of essential questions you'll need to ask yourself before deciding to give your day job the flick.

Envisage your investing journey one year from now. What does your world look like? Have you become a skilled trader, immersed in market knowledge? Have you identified and addressed the gaps that currently hinder your desired results? Think about what your future self would thank you for today.

Visualise who you will be in 10 or 20 years' time. Picture that person in detail. Where do they live? How do they behave? What sort of life are they living? What are their values? If you look to your 'older you' for guidance, you'll be drawn to your ideal life.

If you met your ideal you — your older mentor — face-to-face now, what advice would they have for you? What path would they suggest you choose so you can become your best 'you' over the next decade?

Write down your answers. I think they may surprise you.

Constructing an image of 'future-you' will help you work out what you need to do today to excel in the markets tomorrow.

A small warning about this method: beware of the *arrival fallacy*, the feeling that achieving a particular milestone will bring everlasting happiness. If you've ever caught yourself thinking, 'I'll be happy once I get married ... get that job ... have a baby ...', you may be a victim of this bias. Appreciating the journey is the key, rather than expecting our future achievements will themselves make us happy.

25

3. Break it down

Whenever I face a daunting trading task, like learning a piece of software, or a new brokerage platform, I tell myself, 'Just a quick peek. Yes, that's it—a tiny glance before I can kick back for the day.'

I mean, who can resist reading one more page, one more email, or watching another short video? Who can step away from their computer once they've opened the charting package, or punched in their login details? It's more like leisure than work.

And once I start I get fascinated by the project. Before I know it, I've brainstormed and researched the confusing task at hand, all without breaking a sweat.

My brain falls for this every time. I'm so gullible it's almost comical.

Name the goal you've been procrastinating about, then just take the tiniest first step towards achieving it. Once you get rolling, it'll be done in a flash. It's called the 'foot in the door' technique in psychology. It's genius and I think you'll love it.

It originates from a persuasive method where you start with a small request and follow up with a larger one. If you break down your task into the smallest possible components, then tackle the first one on the list, you're more likely to complete the full list. Here's what to do:

1. Break down each task into small, bite-sized chunks.

2. Reward yourself for achieving even the smallest of these landmarks.

3. Make yourself answerable to a higher authority. For example, ask your partner or your best friend to check up on your progress, every day if necessary.

4. Visualise the rewards that come from completing each micro-step, and dramatise the punishments that will eventuate from not finishing the task.

Change takes courage. It can involve a grieving process when we say goodbye to the old and grapple with the uncertain, frayed edges of the new. Even accepting change takes courage. These three methods can give you the jump start you need.

It's time for action

You can read this book like a novel, for entertainment. Or you can aim to apply what you're learning and change the trajectory of your life and your trading forever.

If you're determined to make changes, pull out a notebook and answer these questions:

1. What habits are you looking to develop outside of the financial markets?

2. What trading habits do you want to develop?

3. Is there a date or event you can use as a fresh start to help you initiate these changes?

4. What does your future self look like — one year, three years, five years from now?

Creating a new habit

There's a lot of research on habit formation. In general, creating a new habit comes down to four things:

1. It must be easy to measure.

2. You must be able to do it frequently or immediately, with a high level of repetition. (This explains why you

have trouble remembering how to change the time on your electronic clocks every time daylight savings ticks around.)

3. It must give you some sort of reward, because unless your behaviour is rewarded you won't repeat it.

4. You must be sure you can do it (a 9 or 10 on the confidence scale). This means you must be absolutely sure you can create this new habit. Jeremy Dean, author of *Making Habits, Breaking Habits*, suggests this is one of the best ways to make a habit stick.

How confident are you that you can develop this habit?

Let's look at an example. Imagine you're trying to remember to brush your teeth in the morning. This is an easy-to-measure outcome; it's something you do frequently and at around the same time of the day. Revelling in the feeling of clean teeth can be your reward. To maximise your chances of this behaviour becoming a habit, you'd need to feel really confident you can do it (a 9 or 10 on the confidence scale).

That's what it takes to create a habit. Then you need to repeat a chosen behaviour until it becomes automatic and effortless. The research definitely backs this, as without repetition the cycle of cue, or trigger behaviour, then reward just doesn't get a chance to take hold.

But problems pop up when things get too complicated.

One of the best mentoring methods is to strip out the complexity. Break a complicated task down into mini-steps. This is the way to accomplish the broader goal. And with the accomplishment of each mini-step you'll be a step closer to achieving what's really important to you.

Unfortunately, our first inclination, after tasting success, is to take the initial idea, and then... complicate it. Don't do this. Focus on the simple steps and habits that give you the biggest gains. These will have the most impact.

Complexity won't lead you to more money. Simplicity and habit formation are the keys to effective trading. Consider an area in your life where you'd like to form new habits so you can put certain aspects onto autopilot. Then use the latest science-backed, data-driven research to help you cement those habits so you can attain a higher level of achievement in your chosen field.

Key concepts

- Develop habits to take the pressure off your working memory and you will have created space for learning new skills.

- Take control of your time, your trading and other priorities in your life so most of the repetitive tasks can be done automatically.

- Make a list of the key habits you'd like to form and make sure they are easy to measure, that they are done frequently or immediately, and that they give you some sort of reward so you'll be happy to repeat them. You also must be confident you can actually do it.

(continued)

- Getting started on developing a new habit can sometimes be the most difficult step. You need tools to encourage you to combat your inherent resistance.

- Harness the fresh start effect, by pinpointing a specific date or event you can use as a cue when starting a new habit.

- Visualise your future self to guide your actions today.

- Break down your desired behaviour into bite-sized actions, remember the importance of a supportive environment, seek support and allow yourself some missteps along the way.

Let's look at some specific habits you need to develop as a trader. Then we'll focus on how you can put these trading habits on autopilot.

CHAPTER 3
Autopilot investing

Maintaining effective habits is like building a muscle. The more you do it, the stronger the habit becomes. Once your habit is strong enough it becomes automatic. And the best part? Eventually that new habit won't take nearly as much effort as it used to. You will become a well-oiled investing machine that runs mainly on autopilot. Here's how to develop exceptional trading habits — fast.

Some people will easily absorb what I can show them about trading. Others will need a complete overhaul, root and branch, before they can grow their equity. For most people it takes time and practice to perfect their skills. But once you have, effective investing becomes second nature. Your brain works smarter. It's the equivalent of having a personal assistant in your head who takes care of all the little things so you can focus on the big picture.

And there's a secret weapon to help you get there faster. It's called *chunking*. First introduced by cognitive scientist George Miller in 1956, chunking happens without your conscious awareness. Your brain groups similar things together so you don't have to remember them all separately. It's like having a cheat sheet for life.

Yes, to begin with, you must exert conscious willpower and create and change your own habits. But that's when the magic happens. A repeated behaviour becomes hardwired in the brain, so your working memory is less overwhelmed and you don't have to exert so much conscious control.

Neuroplasticity

When certain behaviours are linked in your brain, they start firing together automatically. It even shows up on an MRI scan. Neurologists call it 'wiring together, firing together'.

When you repeat actions frequently, your brain's autopilot kicks in and groups this information together in neat little chunks.

And guess what? This brain phenomenon isn't limited to market-related habits. That's why beginner tennis players need to focus hard on every move, while pros make it look effortless. Your brain transforms a series of actions into a smooth routine. This magical process is what lies at the heart of habit formation.

Your adult brain isn't set in stone; it's actually super flexible. This is called neuroplasticity. It's a brain's ability to reorganise and adapt by forming new neural connections in response to learning, experience or injury. Your brain has the incredible ability to change and adapt throughout your life.

Let's have a look at how this can happen. It's related to the connections between neurons, which are called synapses. These little guys can strengthen or weaken over time. Your brain can even transfer the activity associated with a specific function to a different location. That's why so many people who have learned how to trade effectively find other areas of their lives also benefit.

Neuroplasticity shows up in microscopic changes in individual neurons and can also happen on a larger scale, especially in response to injuries. If you want to dive deeper into this mind-bending topic, I highly recommend Norman Doidge's book *The Brain That Changes Itself.*

Sure, some of the childhood habits you develop can stick with you for a long time, but here's the good news: it doesn't mean you're stuck with them forever. Your brain continues to grow and change throughout your life, based on what you actively engage in.

Don't underestimate the power of repetition and practice. If there are habits or behaviours you want to change, you can. Try new activities, repeat positive behaviours and watch as your brain rewires itself to support your desired changes.

What habits should you develop?

You're not bound by past habits. Embrace the growth and plasticity of your brain, and with consistent practice and repetition, you can create new pathways and shape the person you want to become. Let's have a look at the type of habits you should focus on developing.

1. Time management

If you're over the age of 50, you have less than 2000 weekends to go. That is really scary to me. Time runs out quickly, so you need to use your time wisely.

Successful traders have a knack for mastering their time, and you can too. If you don't take charge of your time, others will gladly take it from you. Put on your armour and protect your precious minutes from those sneaky time vampires. Be ruthless about what and who you allow into your life.

Prioritise your own needs, goals and prosperity. Don't let anyone waste your most valuable resource. Identify those time bandits and figure out how to deal with them. I guarantee, if you don't make tough decisions now about where you invest your time, you'll end up with the same results you've always had.

What can you delegate or release to free you up? What habits can you alter to give you back your life?

Politely decline that extra drink after work if it's going to drain your energy. Don't let that negative-talking, chatty relative or friend bring you down and suck up your time.

Set mini-goals with deadlines so you can experience that gratifying rush of endorphins when you achieve them. Celebrate your accomplishments and acknowledge your efforts to reinforce positive behaviour.

Investors are by nature optimistic risk takers. We are confident we can make money. We say yes to risk. We say yes to learning about how to trade effectively. We say yes to a brighter future for ourselves and our family.

I've said yes to a lot of opportunities that paid off:

Geoff Wright, my first publisher: 'Do you want to write a book?'

'Yes.'

Chris Tate, my business partner, in the late nineties: 'Should we start a business together to help traders make more money?'

'Yes.'

Chris Bedford, my husband, in the early 2000s: 'Do you think we should start a family?'

'Yes.'

The list is long.

And my track record of success with yes makes it difficult for me to say no. Sometimes — even now — I say yes when part of me is screaming, 'No! No! No!'

We feel guilty, we want to please. Saying no sometimes hurts. It disappoints others. Most of us are still actively suffering from the Willie Loman complex — the desire to be liked and to be nice.

However, the more opportunities that open up, the more I have to say no. No to the 'sure-thing' tip. No to trading when my signals aren't perfect. No to catching up with my friends when it's my prime markets time.

In short, most multi-millionaire traders say yes carefully, not impulsively, and they say no more often than they'd like.

Maybe you should try saying no a bit more often, and watch your time open up and new opportunities for you to focus on your own priorities blossom. Freud once said, 'One day, in retrospect, the years of struggle will strike you as the most beautiful.'

If you don't take control of your time, others will. Identify any time leaks and take action to address them effectively.

Also consider whether to delegate. Let's assume you work 40 hours a week, and you're an overachiever so you put in 50 weeks a year. That's 2000 hours of paid employment.

If you want to make $100 000 a year, each hour is worth $50. If you want $1 million a year, each hour must be worth $500.

Thinking about getting a cleaner or someone to mow your lawns? If they're charging less than $500 per hour, they're an absolute bargain.

Delegate those parts of your life that take time away from educating yourself about trading. It's the only way you'll be able to fit everything you want into your life without burning the candle at both ends.

2. Trading habits

Here's an easy tip to try. As soon as you've finished this part of the book, open up your electronic calendar and schedule a time to review your trading plan. If you haven't got a trading plan yet, for heaven's sake download my free trading plan template from www.tradinggame.com.au and fix that up as soon as you can.

Trading plans should be revised at least annually, and I'm not talking about endless fiddling with indicators.

Examine your past trades. Aim to understand why you made the decisions you did as a trader, and isolate areas where you could have acted irrationally. What are your sweet spots in terms of the markets and the time frames you trade?

Can you create separate equity curves for each of the markets you trade and each of the time frames you trade? Are there any financial market universes creating friction and dragging down your results? Look for flaws in your process.

During your annual review, keep an eye out for flaws in your process. Imagine if another trader followed your system, would they achieve the same results? If not, your plan just isn't specific enough and needs fine-tuning.

If you've followed your trading plan and made a loss, it's still a 'good trade', because you stayed true to your plan.

It often takes around three years before an investor has developed any level of proficiency, so give yourself time to grow. You're not going to be able to achieve incredible profits in your first year. Many investors quit prematurely, which is unfortunate.

Listen. The pain is temporary. It may last for a minute, an hour or a year, but eventually it will dissipate. If you quit, though, it will last forever, and you'll never escape from the fact that you made the decision to quit.

Young Steve Jobs worked out of his mum's garage.

Young Martin Luther King Jr was nervous about presenting in public.

Benjamin Franklin was called 'slow' by his third-grade teacher.

Charles Dickens left school at 12 to work in a factory after his dad was thrown into debtors' prison.

You'll start out in one place, but that doesn't mean you'll end up in the same spot.

I'm troubled by the imprecise. The fuzzy. The 'open to interpretation'. Imprecision is dangerous. Imprecision is costly. And it is unnecessary.

Banish the 'kind of', 'sort of', 'could be' statements from the vocabulary of your trading plan. Replace these words with the crisp, unambiguous sharpness of precision.

Do this, and you will reap the rewards. Keep developing these success habits and your equity curve will thank you.

And if you need a bit of help with the specifics of trading, you can always refer to my other books, *Trading Secrets*, *Charting Secrets* and *The Secret of Candlestick Charting*. They will all help you create a winning trading plan.

3. Life habits

'But Louise, you don't understand. Unless I can commit 100 per cent to investing, I'm not going to get started.'

Oh come on!

Yes, it sounds admirable, even virtuous. But it's wrong. Dead wrong. No one devotes 100 per cent of their time and energy to trading. Not even full-time traders.

Almost everyone starts this as a side hustle. Something outside their mainstream.

Me? I've always had a side hustle. When I worked full-time, I also worked part-time. That's also when I learned how to trade — when I had two jobs at the same time. When I was at school, I toasted my friends' sandwiches for 20 cents — up against the heater with a contraption I made where I rubber banded a fork to a wooden ruler.

I think the work ethic I inherited has stood me in good stead. And now, as a full-time trader, I enjoy helping others succeed.

Fit in learning to trade around your schedule. It's a worthwhile side hustle that deserves your focus.

Choose a habit to adopt

So far we've covered how habits are formed. Now it's time for you to move the needle in your own life and put some of these findings into practice.

Pull out your notebook and start making plans for a habit you want to adopt or change. Make it a habit that relates to time management, trading or another aspect of your life.

Define exactly what the new habit looks like and make specific plans on how you'll make it an ongoing part of your life.

A common trait among successful people is they start with the end result in mind. If they want to make a million bucks from their business, they set up a business capable of generating that level of profit. It may sound simplistic, but it's a powerful concept. Interestingly, when some traders start out, they short-change their own potential results by not fully committing to their venture.

Embrace the mindset of successful people and envision the income level you desire then set up strategies to support that vision. Don't strangle your own potential.

The fantasies people have about 'being a trader' never fail to astonish me. Otherwise sensible people tell me how much they envy me. 'I wish I could trade for a living,' they tell me. And 'I envy your discipline.'

It's funny how they never say, 'I wish I had your tenacity' or 'I wish I could stick with mundane tasks for decades as you do.' I find that intriguing. But let me tell you, in trading, it's precisely those qualities that matter the most. The ability to persevere, even when you don't feel like it — that's what separates the winners from the rest.

Sure, there are days or weeks when the market seems to shower you with money, and you can't seem to make a wrong move. But that's not when your tenacity is tested. It's when you're not making the profits you think you deserve that the grind of investing becomes real. That's when you need to buckle up and manage it like a pro.

Don't be fooled by the glamorised image of trading. It takes more than wishful thinking and envy to succeed. It takes true tenacity, discipline and the ability to stick with it even when things get tough. As Robert van Eyden, author of *Badass Trader*, puts it, 'Don't treat discipline as a mere option. Treat it as a requirement. Embrace discipline and commit fully.'

Here's the key: you have more control than you think. Develop the right habits to put some aspects of your investing on autopilot. Get your trading plan in tiptop shape then follow it blindly, like a brain-dead zombie (in a good way, of course!).

You need to be clever enough to create a solid plan, but then dumb enough to trust and follow it without hesitation. Effective traders possess a magical blend of ingenuity and a touch of 'stupidity'.

Growth comes from acknowledging our mistakes and taking responsibility for them. By embracing self-reflection and learning from our actions, we pave the way for personal development and avoid repeating the same errors. So give yourself an initial kick, stay open to introspection and let each experience be a stepping stone on your journey to success.

Two top habit hacks

1. The convenience technique

The things you want to become habitual must be convenient for you to do. This is one of the great truths about forming enduring habits.

If you have set up your exercise machine in front of the TV, I'll bet you're more likely to use it than if you stored it under your bed.

Think about how you can make your trading more convenient for you. If your desk is messy, so you can't spread yourself out, or if you haven't got a convenient icon set up on your computer desktop so it takes three button clicks to open your charting package, you'll be less productive.

Every aspect of your life can be made better by making things more convenient. Barriers to your goal create friction, and friction is your enemy.

2. Pair it

Linking one desirable reward to another less desirable activity will reinforce that action and make it more pleasurable.

I listen to my favourite podcasts while I'm at the gym. This makes going to the gym a fun thing to do and has entrenched this good habit in my mind.

Think about what activities you can pair to reinforce that action. It might make all the difference.

Key concepts

- The more specific you can be when you're looking to adopt a new habit, the more likely you'll achieve success. When certain behaviours are linked in your brain, they start firing together automatically. This neuroplasticity will mean your new habits will take less effort and you will act on autopilot.

- Beware of complexity. It won't help you achieve your goals.

- Start with a clear goal and identify a cue or trigger. Be consistent and don't forget to reward yourself. Track your progress, but build in some flexibility in the path to your goal so you can accommodate life's curveballs.

There's a big difference between the way an experienced trader approaches habit development and the way a rookie approaches it. Let's take a closer look at some beginner traders who are 'running with scissors' in the market and what you can do to avoid falling into the same traps.

CHAPTER 4

Three rookie habits hurting your results

Ready to make a fortune in the markets? Your habits could be holding you back. Let's explore three common rookie habits and how to avoid them.

There are loads of books that tell you how to share trade like a champion, raid the markets and make fistfuls of cash. I've written five best-selling books along those lines myself. But it's also good to learn about what *not* to do, so you can avoid things that just don't work.

Beginners almost always make these mistakes, and before you know it they become habits. Let's nip them in the bud, so you can shortcut your way to investing success.

Habit 1: You are cruel to yourself

A trader once told me, 'I hate myself when I make losses in the markets.'

Hmm...well, this is a problem. It could be this is just a one-off case of lousy self-talk. Usually, though, it's a sign of a habitual problem of treating yourself with disdain.

This habit of chastising yourself is a sign of having a fixed mindset. Cultivate a growth mindset to embrace learning and handle failures without undermining your identity.

People with a growth mindset love learning. They use life's lows as ammunition. Their identity isn't threatened when they experience failure.

Be careful about thinking you've achieved all you can achieve in life.

Habit 2: You make things too complex

Yes, a multiple moving average combined with MACD divergence sure looks gorgeous and makes lots of pretty lines on your chart... but how do you use it?

The further you get away from price action, the less evidence there is that *any* of it will bring in one extra dollar. Go for the simple stuff. Make a list of those other brilliantly complex ideas, and save them for later. Go and make some money first.

Unfortunately, for most of us humans, our first inclination after tasting success is to take the initial idea, and then... complicate the bejesus out of it! That's where things start to go off the rails. For over 30 years I've been cleaning up the messes of other traders who have done just that. Force-feeding clarity into chaos. I beg them... beseech them... take them by the shoulders and give them a little shake to get this to sink in: *focus on the simple stuff that works well.*

Don't get lost in the delusion that complexity will lead you to more money. Simplicity and habit formation are the keys to effective investing.

Nearly every trader I know who has made significant funds in the markets has used a simple, elegant trading plan. Then, over time, for some peculiar reason known only to the Investing Gods who take delight in tampering with the feeble minds of mere mortals, they complicate the hell out of everything. This is the most common form of self-sabotage.

I can tell you, adding layers of unproven difficulty, strata of complexity as deep as the Grand Canyon, will do nothing to add to your bottom line. And in the meantime it will crush you.

Usually, the complication is added by someone in a socially acceptable career who has been rewarded in the past for this move towards detail. It's a classic blunder. What happens next is either the trader finds it all so oppressive they want to quit or they end up dicing with burnout.

If you're desperate to find your mojo again, get back to the basics. Keep it simple. Trend going up? Then put on the trade. Use a stop loss. Trail it up.

Before you end up despairing and bereft of hope, look to see where you can uncomplicate your trading plan. See where the bloat is and squish it.

Oh yes, I can feel you resisting this. You're thinking, 'Hell, what would she know?'

Well, you don't have to trust me. But if you stay with me, I bet you'll rise above your self-inflicted wounds and get your groove back sooner than you think.

I speak from personal experience on this, because it's actually one of my own key money blocks. When things get too complicated in my life, and I find the wheels start to fall off, I make mistakes more easily and I'm more likely to burn my hand on the frying pan. It usually means I'm under pressure and I've stopped saying no.

No to adding just those extra five pages to my trading plan.

No to learning about the new market that trades 24 hours a day, which doesn't fit with my family values.

No to the time vampires around me, eager to feast on my most precious resource.

Identify your money blocks

- What's blocking you from making money today?
- What habits have you cultivated in the past that are interfering with your investing?
- Spend some time identifying the cues that trigger you to speak harshly to yourself.
- Where have you made things too complex?
- What areas of your life would benefit if you sought more support?
- What's going to make you the most money with the least effort?

*I hope as I write today, my words seep into your heart
and help inspire you to see the world differently,
to be in the world differently. I hope you can see
yourself as your best self. Focused, disciplined, kind.
And a powerful trader. You.*

Habit 3: You think you can go it alone

Many professionals know finding the right mentor can make all the difference, but too often investing is viewed as a personal and isolating pursuit. Your passion may not be widely understood by the other communities in which you operate — family, work, friendships. So be mindful of who you associate with for support or you'll suffer the consequences.

In many ways my business partner, Chris Tate, and I have acted as each other's mentor. I remember a particular time when Chris was by my side as I was trading. He saw my flustered distress and excitement at the bounty on my screen as a big profit was accumulating (yes, even unexpected profits can cause a stress response). He whispered, 'Remember... be a pig. Be a pig.' In trading circles 'being a pig' means not letting fear make you back away from sticking with a trade that's still trending. If you hang on, you'll have the opportunity to cash in on a larger profit down the track.

Money won't flow into your account consistently. Sometimes only two or three trades make practically my entire income for the year. If you cut those trades off before they ripen, you'll curtail your own success.

Chris's words really helped. They soothed my impulse to grab those profits prematurely, convert them to cash, throw them on the bed and make a money angel while chanting, 'I'm rich! I'm rich!'

(Okay, maybe a little too much self-disclosure there.)

By hanging on to that trade, and sticking with my trading plan, I ended up making one of the biggest profits I've experienced to date. If I had sold out when I had the initial inclination, the profit wouldn't have been anywhere near as impressive.

Find a group of investors who will support you, care for you and nurture you. Recognise the importance of finding the right mentor. The medical profession prides itself on this. The education profession, sportspeople, professionals in various trades and in the corporate world — they all consider mentoring essential. Somehow though, when we burst into investing, we imagine we can go it alone. I can tell you, if you hold onto that as a habitual thought pattern, you're destined to make a bunch of mistakes that won't just damage you financially... they'll damage you emotionally. This is the core reason why I started my mentor program, which has been running continuously as a repeat-for-free course since the year 2000.

It is possible to benefit from the support of a group without suffering from 'compareanoia'. I know some traders find they can be triggered when others are achieving in the markets and they're struggling, but that's why it's essential to continue working on your mindset.

We don't have a safety net. We don't have an employer to bail us out, or government assistance to see us through. We know it's all up to us.

Yes, all the weight is on your shoulders. So get into the habit of associating with other investors in the trenches, otherwise you'll never achieve the returns you desire.

Key concepts

- Aim to make each new habit you choose to adopt as simple as possible, and give yourself time to grow.

- Among the habits you're going to need to let go of are being mean to yourself, making things too complex and thinking you can do it all by yourself.

Well done! You're well on your way to developing psychological fitness. You've focused on building your success habits and winning routines so you can improve your investing. This is the first key, and if you haven't taken the time to write down the new habits you want to establish, now's your chance. Grab your notebook. Write down your goal, when you'll start your habit, why it's important to you and how you'll reward yourself. Then detail how you intend to track your progress, and you'll be charging towards your goals in no time.

Next we'll have a look at the second key you'll need to master so you can improve your psychological fitness.

KEY 2
Emotional mastery

Keep your cool and flourish

Years ago I was working as a nameless cog in telesales. Not glamorous, and very low-paid. I was totally expendable, but I always felt I was destined for better things.

I met my first real trader at that job.

Glen was a lazy salesman who only ever scraped by, yet he always seemed to be loaded with cash. The best suits, the silk ties, the fanciest car ... and the arrogant attitude. He was only a little older than me but radiated smugness, confident of how smart he was.

I was intrigued. I thought, how can you be rolling in moolah but only *just* make your sales target each month?

So I asked him, 'Are your parents really wealthy or something?' He explained that he was a trader and he didn't really need to work. He wasn't working for the money. He only worked a job because otherwise he would get bored (trading really doesn't occupy too many hours of each day) and spend the time tinkering.

'Do you think I could be a trader? I own some shares.'

He looked at me like I'd just farted. 'Forget it, Louise,' he said dismissively. 'It's hard. You'd never figure it out.'

Crestfallen, haughtily put in my place, I could have slunk back to my corner of the dungeon, but instead I allowed his insult to burn. And I harnessed the building rage I felt at being dismissed like that.

I didn't see much of Glen after he left that job, but I thought about him every step of the way in those early years of my investing career. I especially thought about him when I left my job to become a full-time trader.

Take that, Glen, you would-be dream crusher.

Harnessing my anger to focus on my growth was *way* more powerful than any motivational program I've come across since, and I've tried them all.

There's no shame in using negative motivation. In fact, behind the wild success of most traders, there's someone who told them they'd never make it. They just don't usually share those ancient humiliations and put-downs with the general public. It's their secret sauce for growth.

Glen, wherever you are, I want to thank you again for all you've done for me. That throw-away insult kicked me in all the ways I needed to be kicked. And the adventure it launched me on still continues. I wouldn't be who I am today without you.

What about you? Were you once dismissed or insulted in the past so badly you still feel the sting today? The good news is that burning fuel of anger could drive your investing business to the next level. So don't block that negative emotion…feel it, then use it. Be purposeful with how you use your emotions, because mastery in this one area can make all the difference to your success.

In this part of the book you'll learn about how to avoid self-sabotage, how to develop your sense of purpose and why success has less to do with luck than you'd think.

Let's dive into the topic of emotional mastery and learn how to avoid the obstacles on the way to greatness.

CHAPTER 5

The hidden forces behind self-sabotage

Self-sabotage can happen at any stage — when you're starting, or even just after you've made a huge profit. No one is safe. So why does it happen and what can you do about it?

Traders usually self-sabotage when some niggly little pebble is stuck in their subconscious, impeding their progress. Investing is a marathon, not a sprint. Unless you can get your actions in line with your values, you'll find insidious ways of giving money back to the markets you won't even consciously recognise.

Time and time again I've seen how people's money scripts are out of sync with their actions. We focus on this in chapter 10.

The other way people self-sabotage is by engaging in S.A.D. (self-aggressive and destructive) behaviours.

S.A.D. behaviours

When you were a kid, did you ever play 'Stacks On', where one person falls over, then all their friends pile on top of them. Heaps of fun. It turns out this game holds a valuable investing lesson.

Have you been feeling stressed and overwhelmed lately? Often it can feel like Stacks On with problems, can't it? We've all been there!

When we're under pressure we naturally reach out for something to make us feel better. We want a quick fix. A short-term buzz. Something to give us immediate pleasure.

Our 'future self' switches off, because we want to feel better immediately. But those impulsive, mood-boosting activities you turn to might actually be stopping you from dealing with the root cause of your stress.

If you're not careful, those little so-called boosts can just add to your load — and before you know it you feel like you're at the bottom of the Stacks On pile.

S.A.D. behaviours aren't helpful in the long run. You whack yourself in the head with a hammer for no good reason, other than that you believe you have to. You max out your credit card while stressed about your finances, use alcohol to treat anxiety or scroll through social media messages instead of connecting with others. More extreme examples include engaging in forms of self-harm such as substance abuse, gambling, excessive consumption or physically hurting yourself.

For me, turning to chocolate is an early warning sign I'm out of balance. Lots and lots of chocolate. It seems to find its way into my mouth without any conscious intervention. It's one of the habits I notice that tips me off that I'm not dealing with pressure effectively.

These behaviours may provide temporary relief, but they don't solve the issue.

So what can you do? The answer may surprise you.

Consciously add more stress!

It sounds counterintuitive, but intense emotions and pain actually motivate us to make changes and overcome the big stressors quicker.

Allow yourself to feel. Work out until your muscles are completely knackered, or go for a walk that makes you puff yourself stupid.

Or force yourself to do something unpleasant but productive. By embracing stress and becoming aware of our thoughts, we can catch ourselves before defaulting to S.A.D. behaviours. Stress can be a catalyst for change.

So instead of avoiding stress, let's get curious about it and use it to bring long-term happiness.

Throw yourself into learning about investing, even if things are flying out of control. Block off 20 minutes to watch an educational video or read an article that might transform your mood and your investing methods. Then give yourself a pat on the back for moving forward, even if it feels like it's just by one centimetre.

Also, if you want to be in the top 5 per cent or even 1 per cent of income earners, you must be the one to give yourself a pat on the back when the time is right. Don't fall victim to measuring yourself on artificial success. The only type of success in the markets is visible in your bank balance, in your efficiency at following your trading plan and in your personal growth.

What prevents you from getting where you want to be from where you are now is your mindset. One thing is certain: no trader can outgrow or outperform their own mind. Either you're growing or you're stagnating. There is no middle ground.

Anyone who admits to being too busy to read or too frantic to focus on their own self development is about to experience a steep decline in their own personal fortune. No ifs or buts.

Continually seek out ways to work more productively. To achieve more in less time. To improve on your already effective strategies. Put some thought into these issues:

- What warning signs have you noticed that suggest you may be headed for self-sabotage, depression or ill health?

- Can you detect these in yourself early enough to take action?

- What sort of action alleviates your psychological distress?

Leo Tolstoy wrote, 'Everyone thinks of changing the world, but no one thinks of changing himself.'

Traders often do exactly the opposite of what they should be doing. They blame others, procrastinate and are prone to self-sabotage. And in many cases they don't know *why* they act the way they do. Researchers Lo et al. reported, 'We find that subjects whose emotional reaction to monetary gains and losses was more intense on both the positive and negative side exhibited significantly worse trading performance.'

This is compelling evidence. If you ever needed a reason to work as hard on your mindset as you do your own trading plan, it can be found in that key research.

Another way people self-sabotage is by giving up before they reach their goals.

The Kafka effect

Have you ever felt tormented and ready to quit? Felt that fog of unease before you make a complete breakthrough or creative leap?

Well... that's the Kafka effect. It's the fog that sets in just before you reach your goal.

If you're in a fog of confusion, and you've been putting in a lot of effort but getting nowhere, you are probably due for a dynamite breakthrough. The confusion you're feeling is likely to be a precursor to success.

If you're learning about investing and you're worried you might not make it, your brain will be running in overdrive. It will be seeking out creative solutions and making lateral leaps.

You're out of your comfort zone, and that's where the magic happens.

Failing to understand the upside of 'negative' emotions is another obstacle to getting the best out of yourself.

Fear can drive you

Years ago, when I was living the corporate life I sometimes felt very alone. Climbing the corporate ladder, I tried to navigate this unknown territory without the guidance of someone who really cared about my progress. I focused intently on the next promotion, but was unsure of what this would mean to my life... more hours, more responsibility … but not much more pay. Then told it was 'not the right time' as a less qualified, less knowledgeable candidate was chosen for the plum role I'd had my eye on.

Getting up when it was dark, getting home when it was dark — because of the long hours I was working. Robbed of the prime daylight hours, my husband getting only the husk of me instead of the best. I accepted it all like a drone because I didn't know there was a better way.

Sometimes, even now, I wake up at 3 am in a cold sweat, thinking I've missed a project deadline, or I didn't hit my sales target, or I failed an audit. Honestly, it is the stuff of nightmares. Nightmares that must live in my subconscious. Some deep part of me still fears having to go back and get a 'real job' if I mess up as a trader. I think this is one of the main impulses that keeps me loyal to my trading plan.

What drives you? What aspect of fear can you harness in your life to drive you towards your goals?

Fear doesn't always have to be negative. It can motivate you … if you let it. Think about how you can harness your emotions for success in your investing journey. What motivates you, and how can you use it to your advantage?

When does money switch from being a positive to a negative force in our lives?

Of course, self-sabotage can impact other areas of our lives as well as our investing. Think more broadly about how your views about money could be damaging you. Here's how to know whether you've got a problem:

- if money is an obsession — one of the last things you think about before going to sleep and the first thing you think of when you wake up

- if you judge the integrity and calibre of the people you meet by their bank account, their clothes or the car they drive

- if you judge your self-worth by your bank account, your clothes or the car you drive

- if your sense of self is seriously compromised when you either make a lot more money or lose a lot of money

- if you are more concerned with money than you are with your health, your relationships, your engagement in new projects or your pleasure of a night out

- when it negatively impacts your most meaningful relationships

- when money becomes more important than principles.

I don't suggest there is any problem with being seriously wealthy, if that's your goal. However, I am saying that our views about money can sometimes get out of kilter and damage our emotional wellbeing and our relationships.

How do your views about money affect you?

Key concepts

- It's likely you're a step away from self-sabotage in the markets if you are indulging in S.A.D. (self-aggressive and destructive) behaviours.

- Be wary of quitting, because you're probably closer to your goal than you think.

- Recognise that fear can sometimes be your friend. It can keep you safe and inform you when something is truly important to you.

A large part of avoiding self-sabotage is continual reinforcement of healthy mindset patterns. That's why I created my *Trading Psychology Master Class*. This is a full 12-month, week by week life-changing course, designed to get you to perform at the top of your game… whatever instrument you're trading, whatever market method you're following. You can pick up your copy at this link: www.tradinggame.com.au/masterclass.

And I invite you to register for my free monthly newsletter at my website: www.tradinggame.com.au. That way you can keep feeding your mind.

A major way people sabotage themselves is by not focusing on the task they've set themselves. This is probably the most common reason why people give up when they should push forward. We'll look at this issue together in the next chapter.

CHAPTER 6

Regaining focus in a distracted world

Do you find yourself constantly distracted by the digital noise around you? You're not alone. In today's fast-paced world, maintaining focus is a real challenge. You may be a victim of digital overload. Here's how to fix it.

I have a pet peeve: watching my friends and fellow investors drop everything they're doing to pay instant attention to the incessant beeping of their electronic devices. These beeps are intrusions and at war with our privacy, autonomy, focus, productivity and ability to get any project completed. Constant screen use is rewiring our brains, and is the antithesis of relaxation.

It used to be we would be annoyed by a knock at the door or a ringing phone around dinner time. Now it's likely family activities will be unceremoniously interrupted at the first beep, bong or clink of an electronic device.

And it's ruining relationships.

It's ruining our quality of life.

Our devices are designed to hook us like a drug, flooding our brains with dopamine. You know that feel-good neurotransmitter responsible for making you desire and for feelings of being rewarded? According to a study by Peraman and Parasuraman, 'Everyone has to accept that relationships with mobile phones are risky for anyone, and it can steer us into "mobile phone mania" or "nomophobia", a psychological disorder which is equally as dangerous as, and similar to, narcotic drug addictions.'

Think I'm exaggerating? Keep an eye out for it.

If you have meaningful conversations with 10 people over the course of a week, I'll bet at least one of them will have glanced at their device in the time you're with them. It's utterly disrespectful, and it's catching. If they look at their device, you're much more likely to glance at your own.

Sustained eye contact and empathy between people talking together are experiencing a slow death.

Everyone seems to be simultaneously interrupted and interrupting, dropping everything they're doing while trying to get everyone else to drop everything they are doing. Let's face it, you probably won't read all of this chapter in one hit. (Is that a phone ringing? A beep on your computer? A little electronic ping from your phone? Now... what was it you were saying?)

In the age of instant gratification our attention span has withered. We're addicted to quick hits of information, and it's affecting our ability to focus.

A little story

Once upon a time, a big shot named Charles Schwab was too busy to sit through a long, boring presentation by an efficiency expert. So he was like, 'Yo, give me your best tip, dude.'

The expert said, 'Every morning, make a to-do list with the most important stuff at the top. Focus on the first task until it's done, then move on to the next one, and so on. Do this for a month and then pay me what you think it's worth.'

And you know what? Schwab loved it so much, after the month, he sent the guy a whopping $25000 cheque. If it worked for Schwab, it can work for all of us. But the catch is, in today's world of endless distractions, it's increasingly hard to stay focused and get things done.

Blame it on evolutionary biology, but back in the day we needed gossip, drama and art to keep us informed about what was going on in our tribe. Fast-forward to today and we have a constant stream of news and gossip at our fingertips. We're apparently powerless to resist it.

Distraction sickness

Picture this: you're trying to get some serious trading done, but your mind and mouse keep wandering off to cute cat videos and social media feeds. It's called distraction sickness, and it's like a virus that infects our ability to focus and achieve our goals. It's affecting everyone. And because so much of what distracts us is fascinating it's difficult to resist.

If you want to make it big as an investor, you need to learn to beat this beast.

Why's it important?

Without being able to focus and go the distance as a trader, you just won't get the results in the markets you're craving. As with any skilled performance endeavour, there are so many moving parts. However, with good planning, you can get your most important tasks done each day and hit your goals.

Maintaining your focus can be even more difficult depending on the time of day and how you're feeling — tired, hungry or hangry (you know, that state where you're hungry and it makes you angry... or is that just me?).

According to social psychologist Roy F. Baumeister, decision fatigue hits us hardest before lunch and in the late afternoon: 'Even the wisest people won't make good choices when they're not rested and their glucose is low.' But fear not! Taking a break, having a snack or simply resting can help replenish your mental resources and boost your performance.

Even judges in criminal courts are impacted by this phenomenon, it seems. One study found, 'You are anywhere between two and six times as likely to be released if you're one of the first three prisoners considered versus the last three prisoners considered.' The likelihood of a favourable ruling peaks at the beginning of the day and declines steadily over time from a probability of about 65 per cent to nearly zero, before spiking back up to about 65 per cent after the judge has had a break for a meal or snack.

Plan your day. Start strong and tackle your most important tasks first, before decision fatigue sets in. And don't forget to fuel up with a snack or two along the way. Your investing success might just depend on it.

How to stop being a victim of distraction overload

Here are three methods you can use to get focused and avoid the pitfalls of distraction.

1. Guard your environment

If you're serious about crushing your goals, create a success environment. But here's the catch: you've got to identify those sneaky little distractions holding you back. Pay attention to your own behaviour for a day or two and access your personal kryptonite. It could be your phone, your email or even a chatty co-worker. And don't think you're off the hook during brunch with a friend — according to research, leaving your phone face up could be sabotaging your focus and ruining your enjoyment of quality time.

Make a habit of turning off your phone notifications when you're concentrating on a task that demands focus.

Cure your mobile phone addiction

Did you know 62 per cent of people whip out their devices when stuck in line? Shockingly, 80 per cent of people can't last more than 20 seconds without checking their screens. It looks like we've become a society that can't tolerate even a moment of boredom.

(continued)

Studies show that we check our phones an average of 85 times a day, spending about 30 seconds each time. And the worst part is, we don't even realise we're doing it.

It's time to take back control and learn how to focus, especially if you want to succeed in the investing world.

Here are three practical steps to minimise mobile phone addiction:

1. Establish tech-free zones and time blocks: Designate specific areas or times phone use is off-limits, like the bedroom or during meals, to create healthier boundaries.

2. Practise mindful smartphone usage: Before reaching for your phone, pause and reflect on your intentions. Set goals for usage, be aware of app time and make conscious choices aligned with your priorities.

3. Engage in offline activities and hobbies: Discover enjoyable pursuits that don't involve your phone, such as reading, exercising or pursuing creative outlets, to reduce dependence on constant stimulation.

Break free from mobile phone addiction gradually, being patient with yourself and celebrating small victories. Reclaim your time and focus, and live a more balanced life in our hyper-connected world. Take your first step on the journey to regaining freedom from the mobile phone spell.

2. Set aside chunks of time

Block out chunks of time in your calendar for important tasks, and set a timer to let you know when it's time for a break. Need to learn how to use that fancy charting package? Schedule a time slot each week to work on it, and stick to it rigorously. You'll be amazed at how much you can accomplish with a little bit of planning and focus.

And minimise noise. Gary Evans, an expert on environmental stress, discovered noise messes with our learning ability.

When the new and former Munich airports opened and closed at the same time, Evans and his team found strong evidence for noise's negative impact. In this study, Evans assessed the same children three times: six months before the old airport closed and the new one opened, and one year and two years after the airport opening. 'Noise exposure is consistently linked to reading deficits and may interfere with speech perception and long-term memory in primary school children,' Evans reported.

Noise reduction not only helps you concentrate, but according to research, it also makes you a nicer person. This is probably because you're less likely to become distracted. You'll stay more focused on listening to your friend, and concentrating on the task at hand.

Dr Libby Sander, Assistant Professor and Future of Work expert at Bond University even found 'a significant causal relationship between open-plan office noise and physiological stress'. She reports, 'Background noise, noisy co-workers, loud telephone conversations, impromptu stand-up meetings in the middle of the office and interruptions make it very difficult to conduct work that requires concentrated effort.'

Interruptions are the enemy of productivity. A recent study from the University of California at Irvine found it takes around 23 minutes for most workers to regain their full concentration after an interruption. That's 23 whole minutes!

Psychological studies have shown that when you're under high stress, you get dumber. It becomes difficult to remember what you had planned to do, especially when you're under pressure to act.

That's probably why so many people strike trouble if they don't have a written trading plan.

It's also why, when faced with a catastrophe such as a wildfire, so many people don't think to call emergency services. And it helps to explain why 11 per cent of skydiving fatalities are due to parachutists failing to access the emergency chute.

Here's a figure to remember: 75 per cent of people suffer cognitive paralysis leading to complete inaction when under stress.

You have to train for emergencies. Pre-plan. Consider how you'll need to react to a series of losses or one big loss in the markets. The purpose of training is to create procedural memory to guide your actions when your thinking shuts down. It allows you to activate the script.

Read your trading plan. Follow it. You wrote your plan when you were calm and thinking clearly. Trust *that* version of yourself, not this under-pressure, out-of-breath, twitchy version of yourself.

3. Bounce less, concentrate more

Think you can multitask like a superhero? Well, think again. The research shows when we juggle too many things at once, we become less efficient and are more likely to mess up.

Give yourself a solid hour each week to plan out your tasks and figure out how to dodge those pesky distractions. I call this my power hour. You'll be able to stay focused and on track.

Here's the thing: Our attention span is like our bank account. We have a finite amount of money and we need to be careful about how we spend it. So let's take a good hard look at all the areas where we're not performing at 100 per cent of our capacity.

By guarding against distractions, you'll be in a better position to trade like a market wizard.

Mass insanity

Apparently, in the first week of December 1927, more stock was traded on Wall Street than at any other time in history. Large numbers of ordinary folk had mortgaged their homes to buy stock, and in America, $2 out of every $5 loaned by banks was for the purpose of stock purchases. President Coolidge warned that the rise wouldn't continue forever but nonetheless people were swept up in a bizarre mass mania and continued to dig deep to buy shares. People quit their jobs to become speculators. They were hooked on the dopamine rush, fixated on the possibility of winning.

The meltdown began on June 12, 1928. Then, on October 24, 1929, all hell broke loose. In five days, $340 billion (in today's currency) evaporated. On October 29, Winston Churchill, who was visiting Coolidge at the time, glanced out of his hotel window to see a failed trader throw himself off the 15th floor.

Others followed.

The destruction was universal. People from all walks of life had participated in the mass insanity—doctors, lawyers, dentists, teachers, hard-working blue- and white-collar family people.

This pattern has been repeated numerous times since, all of it flying in the face of warning voices.

What I want to argue is that these episodes are no different from the technology-driven, attention-deficit issues affecting the majority in today's 'plugged in' society. And it's being fuelled by the same unchecked emotions that are an effect of every second person being addicted to their electronic devices.

If you're a trader, your time, your attention and your ability to think correlate directly to your bank balance. Lose your concentration, and you will lose your trading abilities, your control and your mind.

Few people have the strength of character required to stand aside from this tidal wave of interruption-based idiocy.

You've got to dig deep. Beat off those distractions. Develop silence in your mind to overcome the background noise while you're trading. Seek quiet contemplation. Allow yourself to think. Fight for it. Your biggest frustrations will be when you have people demanding your attention to fulfil their own agendas. Your best insights will occur in calm. Clarity will be gained. Life choices will become clear.

Key concepts

- Beware of the constant distractions in your life that can harm your focus, productivity, relationships and happiness.

- Consciously create a success environment to guard against distractions and make it a priority to establish boundaries to regain control over your focus.

- Set aside time for deep work even if that means booking an appointment with yourself in your calendar.

Many traders grapple with their identity as a trader. The next chapter will show you how to live according to your life's true purpose and excel in the markets.

CHAPTER 7

Purpose trumps passion

Need proof of how developing your reason 'why' will help improve your performance as a trader? Keep reading to explore this further and to learn how to silence negative self-talk.

I once heard a trader say, 'Oh my gosh, I want to trade full-time so badly. I'm putting in 100 per cent, and I'm going to throw everything I've got at it. This is my passion. I love everything about investing!'

Then I watched in dismay as he fizzled out after a torrent of 12-hour days watching the markets and reading 60 books about how to become a super investor.

I heard another trader say, 'I'm going to learn to trade methodically so in three years I'll be able to donate 30 per cent of the money I earn to helping battered women escape from their dangerous home lives.'

Because their purpose was clear, *that* trader achieved their goal.

And now there are stats to back this up.

Professor Morten Hansen, at University of California Berkeley, surveyed 5000 employees to look at the connection between performance, purpose and passion. He found that people without purpose and passion are in the bottom 10th percentile of performers. And he found that those with high purpose and passion were outstanding performers — in the 80th percentile. Pretty much as you'd expect, hey?

The surprise is that purpose is revealed to be far more important than passion.

Someone who scored low on passion but high on purpose showed a major jump in performance — 64th percentile.

	HIGH PURPOSE	LOW PURPOSE
HIGH PASSION	80th percentile	20th percentile
LOW PASSION	64th percentile	10th percentile

Perhaps part of the reason is that purpose connects us to others. So develop your *why*. Even if you don't love every aspect of investing, if you have a firm purpose, you'll come out a winner in the end.

Oliver Wendell Holmes observed, 'Every now and then a man's mind is stretched by a new idea or sensation, and never shrinks back to its former dimensions.'

Once the importance of purpose really gets into your core, you will see everything in a new light.

According to a Princeton University study, emotional wellbeing and happiness increase with wealth — up to a point. However, if your income is over $75000, and you're still blaming lack of money for your unhappiness, then it's time for a re-evaluation. More money isn't likely to make you much happier.

I think that's why I find chasing personal meaning has much more of an impact on my happiness level than chasing the almighty dollar. When my *only* goal is money, I know I've got a problem, and I won't have the energy to drive through. My goals have to hit other hot buttons. Unless I can inspire others by leading by example, the attainment of my own goal seems hollow and meaningless. That's the thought that drives me, and without honouring that aspect of my personality, I get jaded.

The bliss zone

The bliss zone is what I call the unique combination of passion, skill and money that fits you like a glove.

If you have passion and skill, but that activity is not earning you money, then you have a hobby. If you have skill and money but no passion, then you're in a zombie zone (and that's where a lot of people find themselves, pursuing a career that doesn't get their blood pumping). If you have money and passion but no skill, then you've probably just described your boss at work (if they were promoted too quickly).

Think about how you'd define your own personal bliss zone. To me it's where I combine my passions, I'm pushed to the limit (but not past my limit) in terms of my skills and I'm paid brilliantly for my efforts.

This sums up trading and investing beautifully.

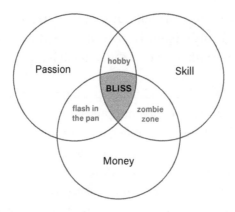

The role of hope

Financial uncertainty looms over most of us. But within all this chaos, there's a little something called *hope*.

Hope is a secret weapon. It can lift us up when we least expect it. Let's take a trip back to the 1950s when a brilliant scientist named Curt Richter conducted a rather peculiar experiment. He took a bunch of rats and plopped them into buckets of water. (Not the most glamorous fate for a rat, I know.) Anyway, these little fellas hoped to swim their way out of the bucket, but there was no escape. On average, they lasted about 15 minutes before giving up and sinking into watery oblivion.

But here's where it gets interesting. In the second round of this rat race (pun intended), Richter rescued the struggling swimmers just as they were about to call it quits. He dried them off, let them rest for a bit and then, without warning, he threw them back into the water. And something incredible happened. The rescued rats swam their little hearts out for a further, whopping 60 hours. That's a mind-boggling leap from 15 minutes!

Our mindset can make all the difference. When we truly believe our circumstances are temporary and that change is possible, we are capable of achieving extraordinary things.

Hope is the magical ingredient that tips the scales in our favour. So hold on tight to hope.

Psychologists have been referring to this experiment for ages because it highlights the power of hope. Believing brighter days are ahead will help you go the distance in the markets, and the longer you stay in the arena, the more likely you are to experience success.

Lessons from Jerry

I'm a big fan of Jerry Seinfeld. He makes it all look so easy. Effortless. Joke after joke delivered so fresh you'd think he makes it all up on the spot. Most people don't realise the massive amount of work Jerry puts in before he sets foot on the stage. Heck—I heard he took two years perfecting one joke!

He's no stranger to honouring his process. Every joke he has written has been plotted out on a yellow pad, using the same type of pen.

He says, 'In my world, the wronger something feels, the righter it is.'

And it hit me like a lightning bolt. For 99 per cent of people, it's unfathomable to work on *anything* with that level of tenacity. People usually give up when they hit the most minor of inconveniences and lack the staying power to stick to their goals. Yet with investing I'm asking you to do just that: work at something consistently so you can achieve a long-term reward blocked off to others who are always on the lookout for shortcuts.

I'd argue the more you can cement your *why*, the more likely you are to be resilient, overcome obstacles, work harder and become a successful trader. And the enemy of purpose is negative self-talk. We so often talk ourselves out of achievement — it's time to silence that undermining voice.

So how can you develop your purpose?

Here are four specific ways you can develop a compelling purpose.

1. Write it down

The investors I've trained who have a clear grasp of *why* they're investing do best. I challenge you to write down 20 reasons why being in the markets is important to you. My guess is you'll struggle after listing the first five, but that's okay. I want you to dig deep. The more clearly you can articulate why this game is important to you, the better off you'll be.

Ideally, your purpose will involve more than just goals for yourself. Aim to involve your vision for your family, your community and maybe even support of a charity you care about. Research suggests external goals promote emotional mastery.

Okay, I'm about to say something controversial. Many people haven't achieved their goal because they've become myopic, short-sighted and — there's no way to put this subtly — *selfish*. All they're thinking about is themselves.

If you've ever asked yourself, 'What will people think of me?' or 'Do I know enough?' or 'Am I good enough?' or 'Am I ready?' or, the most insidious of all, 'Am I worthy?' — then you could be falling into a vicious trap. The trap of considering things only from *your* point of view.

Could it be you've forgotten to serve? Rather than asking self-serving questions, ask, 'How will the outcome help others?' and 'What difference will this make in other people's lives?'

To move forward, develop a greater awareness of why you're doing this.

You'll jump back into service as if by magic, and it will swing your brain over from your own petty concerns into thinking about how to help others. This is a powerful place to be, and nothing is more motivating than running towards your goals because of the impact you'll make on society, your friends or your family. It will keep you focused when it would be easier to veg out on the couch.

There's a bigger game to play, so get over your own stuff and help the people who need your assistance.

That's what leaders do. They do the difficult work, even when they're unsure of the outcome.

I discovered the hard way that no amount of external success could fix the way I felt inside. The more I achieved in my corporate life, the more I felt I needed to achieve. No matter how much I accomplished, I felt a gnawing sense of emptiness.

What are those voices inside your head saying? Is it like you've woken up with a radio blaring inside your brain, feeding you a constant stream of negativity?

'I don't fit in.'

'I'll never make it as a trader.'

'I'm going to have to work until I'm 90.'

Crazy, negative, self-defeating messages stoke our fear that we are not good enough.

Your voices might be slightly different but they're likely to be driven from the same emotion: fear. And yes, as I have suggested, those voices may be there to protect you, to keep you safe, but they can also keep you rooted in a reality you're not happy with.

The first step is to become aware of them, to analyse them. The second step is to change their accent, tone or pitch, until you can laugh at them.

Often their tone is that of a disapproving parent. Change that voice to Donald Duck's and you'll neutralise the voice's authority over your life. Prevent it from powering your reality, and then... then you'll be able to choose your own future.

2. State what you're feeling

State why you feel the way you do, and explore any sources of shame, guilt, embarrassment, sadness or grief. Do you feel shame because you made a mistake? You didn't follow your trading plan, or perhaps you feel you let your spouse down? Can you identify whether this is triggering earlier memories?

Hear how you address yourself, and make an effort to notice when you're heading down a path of self-degradation. The shame you feel is associated with a particular behaviour or event; it isn't part of who you are at your core. Because we're social creatures, our sense of shame serves to keep us in line with group norms. If we step out of line, and try something different, like trading for a living instead of becoming the doctor our dad wanted us to be, it feels like we're taking a huge risk. The potential of being alienated from our group is scary. And we wonder why the decision to trade can feel so monumental!

Often traders who feel shame confuse their behaviour with *who they are* as a person. Your behaviour needs to improve if you're not following your trading plan but it doesn't mean you're bad at your core. It is essential you recognise this because shame depletes you and takes you away from your purpose.

If you're in the hole, know that sometimes you need to get down into the depths to recognise the potential heights you could reach. What emotions are you experiencing right now?

Note any negative emotions of jealousy or comparison. They'll often reveal what you wish you had personally achieved.

Take it to the extreme. Ask yourself, 'What am I willing to die for?' This question often distils our priorities.

3. Be gentle with yourself

See if you can replace your negative self-talk with compassion. Talk to people you trust and get support. Often when we open up about a problem we find others have felt the same way.

Your feelings don't just *land* on you. You generate them.

So if you can generate sad feelings, you can also generate energising, happy ones.

The key is to catch your negative emotions before they spiral into toxic shame. According to Taylor Draughn, if you are really debilitated by feelings of worthlessness and self-loathing, you may need to seek help to escape from its grip. Finding a friend or a professional you can talk to may be exactly what you need in order to move on.

If you've hit a rough patch in the markets, and it all seems too much, know that every successful trader has gone through this and has managed to persevere and ultimately triumph. Success can take longer to achieve than we first think, but that's okay.

You've had beautiful days before. They will come again. In this moment, you can choose new thoughts. Direct your focus towards supporting your own growth.

4. Write your mission statement

All this deep thought is designed to lead to your creating a personal mission statement that will guide your life.

When I was 19 I wrote down my life's mission statement, little realising those simple words would guide my life and provide me with the direction I needed when things got tough. This is what I wrote all those years ago:

'To inspire others by leading by example. To create wealth and spread my wealth to those I love and those I choose. To nurture others to discover their true energy so they can change the world.'

There are a few things there I want to define.

By true energy, I meant the thing you can do effortlessly. These days, people call it 'flow' or being 'in the zone', but I didn't know those terms back then.

I've since read Mihaly Csikszentmihalyi's book on this. In *Flow — The Psychology of Optimal Experience*, he explains how, when you're in a flow state:

- an hour can pass in the blink of an eye

- you feel what you are doing is important

- you're not self-conscious

- action and awareness merge

- you feel in full control

- the experience is intrinsically rewarding.

To create a flow experience:

- you need to be internally motivated

- the task should stretch your skills to their limits, but not to an extent that makes you feel anxious

- there should be clear short-term goals that will contribute to what you are trying to achieve

- you should get immediate feedback on how you are doing.

So, yes, you can achieve flow while investing, when it fulfils the qualities Csikszentmihalyi outlines.

Once I'd worked out how to trade, I needed to spread the word to enable others to use trading as a liberating tool. I wanted success with significance — not just for myself, but for others.

Have you decided to believe in your calling? The Latin verb *decidere* means to cut away. You might need to cut away some parts of your behaviour that you can no longer afford to indulge. And as soon as you've worked out investing is for you, these thoughts will be confronting.

You may have to cut away some television time so you can study. You may have to cut away some self-doubt so you have the courage to persist when things seem confusing.

But when you decide, when your awareness has shifted and you've made that decision, the opportunities will start to line up.

It's one thing to hear your heart whisper which direction you need to take; it's another to believe it and act on it. Do you know in your gut you will be a trader? Have you been denying that part of yourself because it just seems too hard?

Your mission statement should reference your highest values so those values will guide your mission and your actions.

To join the ranks of elite traders, take time out for some serious reflection. Think of what makes you tick as a trader, as well as the benefits you'll enjoy when you conquer this game. How will this help you as well as the people you care about?

Key concepts

- Develop and articulate a clear understanding about why you want to be a trader.

- Realise that those who have cultivated a clear sense of purpose are likely to outperform those who aren't so sure of their future direction.

- Monitor your self-talk and separate your behaviour from your core identity.

- Identify negative thoughts fuelled by fear, emotions of shame or past triggers.

- Move away from self-centred thinking and focus on serving others.

- Show yourself some compassion and work on a personal mission statement based on your personal values.

A voice in our head might whisper that only lucky people rise to the top. Let's see if we can silence that voice once and for all...

CHAPTER 8
Isn't it all just luck?

Are some people just born lucky? You're about to find out…

In 2004, Candy Adams, a lucky single mother, won $10.5 million in the Ontario lottery. What did that windfall do for her life, her goals and her values? Surely she parlayed it into incredible success?

Well… no.

After becoming a millionaire overnight, she spent all that lovely money on designer clothes, parties, vacations and luxury cars. She lived the high life… for a while. It gave her a few fun years, that's for sure. But after less than a decade the fun was over and she went back to living in a rented house and riding the bus to her part-time job. Not a cent left to show.

Candy's story teaches us that wealth is about mindset, and not just the money you have.

Are some traders born lucky? What about you? Do you even believe in luck?

This curiosity led psychologist Richard Wiseman to embark on a fascinating journey. He delved into the lives of over 400 men and women, from doctors to factory workers, who identified themselves as either lucky or unlucky. His aim was to unravel the truth about the notion that some people are just lucky. In one intriguing experiment, Wiseman handed his research subjects a newspaper and asked them to count the photographs.

Surprisingly, the self-described 'lucky' folks finished the task in seconds, while the 'unlucky' ones took an average of two minutes.

Sounds like a case of superior counting skills, right? Well, not quite. You see, hidden on page 2 of the newspaper was a bold message: 'Stop counting. There are 43 photos in this newspaper.' Luck, it seems, is a matter of perception and of paying attention to the fine print.

The 'unlucky' individuals were so fixated on their counting mission they overlooked crucial details and failed to gather relevant information. This pattern of missing key facts was recurrent.

It may appear that luck is a coveted trait for investors, but it's not an elusive superpower reserved for a chosen few. In fact, there are actionable steps you can take to tilt the odds in your favour and invite luck to accompany you on your investing journey.

1. Be aware of the concept of target lock

Target lock is a military term. It describes how a suitably equipped radar system will automatically track a selected target. When a missile locks onto its target, the outcome is clear-cut: it either hits or misses. However, traders cannot afford such a narrow perspective.

It is crucial to examine your trades from multiple angles, so you'll only enter into high-probability positions.

Traders who expand their thinking beyond the single goal of making money can make well-informed decisions and determine whether a particular trade presents a favourable opportunity.

Mark Douglas explains this in his book *Trading in the Zone*. He urges traders to develop a 'thinking strategy' with the aim of achieving a consistent trading performance. It's less about how you perfectly predict the market and more about how well you understand yourself while trading: 'Ninety-five percent of the trading errors you are likely to make — causing the money to just evaporate before your eyes — will stem from your attitudes about being wrong, losing money, missing out, and leaving money on the table.

'Why,' he asks, 'do you think unsuccessful traders are obsessed with market analysis? They crave the sense of certainty that analysis appears to give them. Although few would admit it, the truth is the typical trader wants to be right on every single trade. He is desperately trying to create certainty where it just doesn't exist.'

We all make choices. Some are easy. Some are hard. Some are just plain wrong. To succeed, you must ignore instant gratification and concentrate on the actions you can take to reach your goals.

The trouble is, we can cheat a little on our dreams every day, and no one will notice. Such cheating becomes a habit, and before you know it another day has slipped past.

I'm not perfect on this. Sometimes I vague out, or forget to check my list of 'must dos', and a morning slips by. I take the easy option, do the fun stuff first instead of last. You know what I'm talking about.

Many traders approach temptation to break their rules with a very narrow mindset. For example, 'Just this once, I won't set a stop loss on my new position' or 'Just this once I won't follow my trading rules.' It won't matter if they give in to temptation 'just this once'.

Howard Rachlin, a Professor of Behavioural Economics at Stony Brook University, argues that for any self-control dilemma that relies on your personal willpower to make the optimal choice, there is a way to make that choice a lot simpler.

He found broadening the framing of a task can improve the probability you'll stick with your rules.

What would happen if you *always* broke your rules? Then why are you going to break your rules this one time?

This will help you resist the natural tendency to give in to temptation or take the easy way out. Rachlin defines a concept called patterning. Other scientists have called this same concept choice bundling.

Have you spelled out your trading plan to the point that it covers every contingency? Could you apply the rules you have constructed in every circumstance?

Can you use the thought that if you break your rules once, then you'll have to use that new behaviour always, forever — as a way to compel you to stick to your investing rules?

This kind of framing can help you stick to your trading plan and ultimately, with repetition, develop effective success habits.

2. Be fully present

If you're fully present, you'll be more likely to see signals others may miss.

Effective investors immerse themselves in this field. The concept, called deep work, was introduced by Cal Newport in his book of the same name. Deep work involves maintaining total focus on a cognitively demanding task without being distracted.

For an investor, staying present is crucial. Here are some strategies to encourage traders to remain in the moment — along with a couple of warnings:

- **Meditation.** Regular meditation practices can help you stay focused on the present, enhancing awareness, reducing stress, and helping you make more objective decisions. (It isn't for everyone, though. Recent studies suggest some individuals can experience adverse effects. For example, anxiety and depression may be exacerbated. So this isn't an across-the-board fix. I suggest you try it out and see whether it works for you, but be prepared to monitor your own outcomes before committing to extensive practice).

- **Set clear goals.** Defining specific, achievable investing goals keeps you grounded and attentive to your trading plan. It's easier to stay present when you know exactly what you're working towards.

- **Use stop-loss orders.** Automated orders allow you to limit potential losses by setting predefined exit points, and this reduces the need for constant monitoring. It frees up mental space so you can focus on current market conditions.

3. Create opportunities

Wiseman's research reveals that lucky individuals possess an ability not only to recognise opportunities but also to actively create them. For example, lucky people seek out diverse groups to engage with at social gatherings. They step out of their comfort zone and embrace new experiences, while the unlucky tend to cling to familiar routines and resist change.

To enhance your investing skills, it is crucial you cast a wide net and embrace a broad perspective on opportunities. Surround yourself with a diverse range of people and expose yourself to different ideas. Be open-minded and willing to listen to individuals whose beliefs and strategies in life and in the markets may differ from your own. Embracing other mindsets will allow you to learn and grow, maximising your potential as a trader.

Even if you're not the most outgoing person, you can still listen, read and watch, exposing yourself to ideas that challenge your existing beliefs. The key is to pay attention and seek out things that differ from the norm.

Many people dream of skydiving, but few get to the point of strapping on a parachute. When you get to the point of jumping, you will want to be 100 per cent sure you have acquired the necessary knowledge and have a good support team.

Trading is just like that. So many people dream of doing it. Of those who take the leap, few prepare for it properly.

The old adage that luck is where preparation meets opportunity may not stray far from the truth.

Key concepts

- Traders who evaluate opportunities based on probability and expand their thinking beyond just making money are the ones most likely to succeed.

- Minimise distractions and cultivate deep work to be fully present during trading sessions.

- Stay open-minded and avoid the target lock that may lead you to overlook opportunities.

- Meditation practices are not productive for everyone. Be prepared to experiment to find the tools that work best for you.

A lot of success in this field involves thinking realistically about the markets. Objectivity is essential. In the next chapter, we'll look at how you can develop objectivity.

CHAPTER 9

How to develop objectivity

Objectivity. For investors, it's right up there with oxygen. Unless we can see the markets with clarity, we're unlikely to make money from them. Here's how to ditch extreme thinking and harness the power of objectivity.

When it comes to regulating your emotions, it's important to understand why you feel and act the way you do. Understanding can sow the seeds that will allow you to discover how to regulate your behaviour in order to become a successful investor.

We've already talked about the perils of extreme ways of thinking. Two of the most common are:

- Everything is awesome.

- Everything is awful.

These two ways of thinking can permeate your world view. When you're in the 'everything is awesome' state, you may look around you and see perfection in every aspect of your life. You're filled with optimistic exuberance. The sky is sparkly blue, and the grass impossibly green. Every potential position you see in the markets seems like it could take you to the moon. Each new investing idea seems brilliant and flawless, guaranteed to bring you riches. You believe in yourself so fully it seems nothing stands in your way. Failure is impossible.

On the flipside, when you're in the 'everything is awful' state, dark clouds loom on the sunniest summer's day. You are beset by intractable problems. The lens through which you see the world seems permanently scratched, and even minor issues seem like giant obstacles. When you're in this state as a trader, you doubt yourself, your trading system, and every aspect of your ability to learn about the markets.

The research tells us we are prone to binary thinking: it's a natural tendency known as cognitive distortion, which encourages black and white thinking.

Mood tunnels

Jeff Warren, a meditation teacher and writer, calls these two extreme ways of seeing the world 'mood tunnels'. The tunnel you're trapped in can make it difficult to see the world in any other light.

Emotional objectivity is found at the pivot of the seesaw between these two opposing ways of framing your world. As a trader, the goal of being calm, objective and balanced should be your focus. In a balanced emotional state, you can view opportunities objectively and assess them from a neutral stance. You're likely to use data to inform your investing decisions and follow the wisdom of your written trading plan or checklist. But when you're trapped in one or another mood tunnel, it can be almost impossible to maintain your equilibrium.

Confusing your inner feelings with your perception of the outside world can have a negative impact on your behaviour.

What's the solution?

Here are three techniques you can experiment with to help you establish a balanced mindset and inch closer towards objectivity:

1. Develop mindfulness

Mindfulness is all about staying in the moment and being fully present. It requires paying close attention to your thoughts, feelings and the world around you without judgement. It's a practice used for reducing stress, increasing self-awareness and finding a sense of inner peace. It can involve breaking a task down into micro actions, and paying attention to each, one at a time.

This is a great technique for those new to the markets. However, if you're already excelling with your investing methods and results, stay with what's working for you. One study found that 'the positive contribution of mindfulness on stock trading performance is only present for those with high impulse control difficulties. Surprisingly, mindfulness appeared to lower trading performance of traders who did not have impulse control difficulties'.

Psychologists Daniel Gucciardi and James Dimmock of the University of Western Australia took 20 expert golfers and put them through their paces. Their performance was measured under a variety of circumstances. Some were instructed to think consciously of a detailed set of rules, and focus on their every move. Others were given a single word to think about, such as 'best' or 'smooth', for example. The rest were left to their own devices.

The results indicated that if you focus too much on the individual building blocks of your performance, this will adversely affect the outcome. However, if you focus on a single word or idea that sums up the way you'd like to perform, you'll be a clear winner.

For example, regardless of your level of experience, a primary goal must be to aim for 'consistency'. Unless you execute your trading plan consistently, you will never achieve the success you're aiming for.

Try repeating the word 'consistency' before you sit down to trade, and whenever you feel like you're about to get the yips. Don't think about anything else. Just think about the incredible power of this word. It might just work the magic you need to stay loyal to your trading plan and become a sharemarket winner.

Before you next sit down at your computer to trade, close your eyes and take a deep breath. Notice and recognise your mood.

The goal is to label the emotion you're experiencing. It can be difficult at first but it will become easier with practice. You'll get better at noticing the cues that could suggest you're in one of those mood tunnels.

If you find yourself in a mood tunnel, get curious about its impact. How is this mood manifesting in your body? Get granular. Can you detect a tightness in your shoulders or a constriction in your throat? Is the mood you're experiencing shifting you away from neutrality when looking at the markets and examining your portfolio?

These are significant questions, though the answers may not be immediately apparent.

Sometimes it can help to ask yourself, 'Am I relating to my life from a neutral position, or has a mood tunnel shifted my thinking?'

Recognise it

Your trading behaviour could be influenced by your mood. This is the essence of self-awareness. Once you become aware that you might be in a mood tunnel, the authority of that tunnel is, if only slightly, undermined.

You'll notice you've made a shift. If you are *in* a mood', you'll realise this mood can move through you without altering your behaviour in either a euphoric or a depressive direction.

By noticing and defining your emotions, you create some distance between your sense of self and what you're experiencing. This is a significant step towards developing objectivity.

2. Consciously challenge your perceptions

Initially, as you develop higher levels of self-awareness, the goal isn't to alter the emotions you're feeling. The key here is to acknowledge them. Then you can challenge the feelings. Ask yourself, 'Well, is this necessarily true?'

Often this process will give you specific insights. It is at the core of the counselling method called cognitive behavioural therapy. You might recognise that you over-trade or become overconfident when you're feeling incredibly exuberant about life. Or, if you're weighed down by your problems, you may discover you miss market signals that would qualify as a buy according to your trading plan. A trading plan is a promise you make to yourself. If you don't keep that promise, why would you keep your word to other people?

Heard of the Dunning Kruger effect? In a nutshell, it's what happens when the stupid are too stupid to realise they're stupid. We've all known people who are confident about their capacity to operate in an area in which they are completely unskilled. This cognitive bias helps to explain why such people remain incompetent. The unskilled and overconfident don't see the need to educate themselves, or to improve their skills.

> *In the markets, those who are overconfident end up over-trading. And over-trading leads to lower returns, a big adrenaline dump and chasing after entertainment instead of profits.*

So what if you're experiencing self-doubt and you're wondering whether you can be a trader? You're right on track, ready to soak up the knowledge you know you lack and likely to attain exceptional results.

3. Focus on gratitude

I just got back from the gym. Feeling immense gratitude for my life. Gratitude for the sunlight, for the ability to move my body, for the freedom I am experiencing.

I'm settling back at my desk after some fantastic time away. I can hear my husband whistling happily as he lives his own version of bliss. My kids are at school and uni, revelling in what they're learning, and I'm about to open up my charts and see what the trading world will reveal to me.

I've got incredible new clients to share my life with, as well as loyal clients who have been by my side for the past three decades. Clever clients who I have helped achieve in the markets, as well as in life.

I feel the fullness of it all. I realise if I had made different life choices many, many years ago, my life now would be utterly different.

What are you grateful for in your life? What puts a smile on your face and allows you to revel in your unique specialness? And what can you do to increase experiences like these for yourself today?

Traders find it harder to feel gratitude when they're feeling trapped in the 'everything is awful' mood tunnel. We so often fixate on things we don't have. By diverting our attention to the many things we *do* have, we can invite feelings of happiness, connection and objectivity back into our life.

Let's face it, the world seems to be getting angrier. More people are short-tempered, ready to fly off the handle. Whether it's caused by too much caffeine, a scary housing market or snarled traffic, many people are on a short fuse.

As a trader aiming for emotional stability in all aspects of your life, you can't allow yourself to be drawn into the dramas that surround you. What you experience in one area of your life often leaks into others, as ink is absorbed by blotting paper.

You must be the voice of reason and respond calmly and with a smile while the angry yahoos throw their faeces.

Create a gratitude practice to help downregulate any strong feelings of lack. Try using a gratitude jar: think of all the wonderful things in your life, write them on slips of paper and put them into a jar. When you need a boost, you can look at one of these as a reminder.

Use this same idea by writing objectivity messages about the markets, or quotes from famous traders, and put these into a jar to be read when needed most. Use them as inspiration so you'll be in the right mindset before you place your first trade for the day.

You can take this one step further by asking a friend to be your gratitude buddy. Once a day you could send each other a text or an email quoting one of the reminders you've written from your gratitude jar. Or, if you'd prefer not to involve a buddy, keep a gratitude journal in which you jot these down each day.

Objectivity is a habit that can be cultivated with deliberate effort. Next time you find yourself in a mood tunnel, try one of these techniques. With practice, the wild swings of your emotions will lessen, and you'll trade from the perspective of calm objectivity, which of course should be the goal for every trader.

Key concepts

- Recognise cognitive distortions. Binary thinking, which sees everything as either amazing or terrible, is a common pitfall. Actively challenge these mood tunnels and strive for a more balanced perspective in your analysis.

- Embrace a calm and still mind and you'll gain the ability to observe your emotions and thoughts without being swept away by them. This heightened self-awareness allows you to make investing decisions from a place of objectivity, relying on data and exercising discipline as you follow your trading plan.

- Harness gratitude. By focusing on the things you're grateful for, you direct your attention away from negativity and scarcity. This positive outlook enables you to approach the markets with a clear and balanced mindset, free from excessive optimism or pessimism.

It's time to move on to Key 3—Money mindset. Understanding your own investor personality can unlock the secrets of effective investing.

KEY 3

Money mindset

Know yourself to boost your profits

I remember, many years ago, getting to the cash register with a trolley load of shopping. I handed over my debit card...and the machine rejected it. Oh far out, there wasn't enough money in the account! I thought there was more. I had lost track of my income and expenses, and I was in trouble. I flushed hot with embarrassment.

I'm not proud of this, but I ran. I grabbed my useless debit card, left the full trolley and high-tailed it out of there.

Nothing like lack of money for shrouding you in shame.

That was a turning point for me. My income had dropped, but my spending habits hadn't changed. Maybe you've been in the same boat?

Sometimes it takes a snapping point like this to grab your attention and teach you more about yourself. A lot of success in the markets comes down to self-awareness, so if you can learn more about yourself, it follows you'll have an easier time in the markets.

In fact, knowing yourself is one of the keys to success.

In this part of the book you'll learn about money scripts — the beliefs and attitudes we hold about money. Because these are often shaped by our upbringing and experiences, you'll learn how to raise money-wise children and whether there's a genuine gender gap in trading. And you'll discover tips for keeping your relationships on track when your views about money differ widely from those of your partner, relatives or friends.

CHAPTER 10

Your money scripts could devastate you

Your ideas about money can make or break you. What can you do when you and your partner, relatives or friends are on different pages when it comes to a money mindset?

Did you know that arguing about money is a predictor of divorce? Dr Sonya Britt-Lutter, one of the authors of a study involving 4500 couples, reports, 'Arguments about money are the top predictor of divorce. It's not children, in-laws or anything else.'

Other studies (controlled for income, debt and net worth) replicate these findings. It seems it's universal. And those with less money don't argue about it more than those with more. It happens at all levels of the financial scale.

The problem is not confined to couples. If you're single, you'll still want to read this chapter, because similar arguments can arise within families and across friendship groups. You may face the battle within yourself. So don't switch off because sometimes I'll frame the lessons in this chapter around couples. It may even help you understand your friends' relationships.

Money can bring out the worst in people. When it comes to arguments about money, harsh language is common. Money arguments last longer than other disagreements, they are more intense and the participants take longer to recover.

Unsurprisingly, then, the more arguments about money a couple has, the lower their relationship satisfaction is likely to be.

Conversations to have with your spouse

Do you hide the trades that aren't going well from your partner and only show them the ones where you're making money?

Are you a perpetual bull or a perpetual bear in your conversations with your partner?

Do you deluge your partner with details about investing until their eyes glaze over and they start looking feverishly around the room for a stapler with which to staple themselves to death?

All of these issues may mean that your partner is just not that into you... as a trader.

Often we barrage those we love with things that interest us — never stopping to wonder whether they're as keen on the topic as we are. Take pity on your partner. Give them a break. Find a trading friend to rave to, or you might find yourself damaging your relationship.

At the same time, if your relationship is to flow smoothly, you'll need to have some money conversations. Here are some initial topics:

1. How much can each of you spend before consulting the other?

2. Is 'my' money 'our' money? How do you decide who is responsible for which bills?

3. What level of spending is acceptable as a ratio of what you're each earning?

4. How do you reward yourselves when things go well?

5. And because your past affects your future, what has happened in the past with money that you should discuss, and what are you aiming for in the future?

Start by having these direct conversations with your partner, and you'll be one step ahead. Most fights about money come from a mismatch in expectations. Unless you have a healthy understanding of, and respect for, your partner's perspective, ugly fights can result.

Are you a saver or do you spend everything you earn? Is money about security or do you use it to impress those around you? How long has it been since you talked about these issues with your life partner?

Here are some other ideas for useful conversations. I dare you to bring up a few of these topics over dinner tonight:

- Shall we splurge on a new car or a holiday?

- Are we going to choose private or public schools for our children (and possibly our grandchildren)?

- Are the kids going to university or straight into the workforce?

- Which of us handles the money?

- How much money can we spend on an independent purchase before discussing it together?

- Should we be saving for the future or spending now?

- At what age should we plan to retire, and what lifestyle should we hope for?

- How much shall we plan to give to charity?

By discussing these ideas openly you're more likely to synchronise on your values and priorities.

But what about investing? Have you sat down with your partner and explained it all to them, describing what you're doing and why?

We all crave understanding. 'If only my partner understood me, my life would be complete' or 'If only my partner liked trading, I'd really be able to fly.' Well, have you fully and clearly shared your mind, or are you simply assuming they know?

Have you told your partner that investing is serious for your combined future and you're determined to make your mark? Or have you described it as a hobby that doesn't matter that much?

What we put out into the world tends to be reflected back. But if your partner still isn't on the same wavelength after you've told them what's cooking in your life, they may just be on a different path when it comes to money.

And that's okay! It's not up to you to coerce them into taking your point of view.

Let them come to their own understanding of the role of money in your life, and for goodness' sake don't fall into 'mentionitis', where everything you talk about relates back to the markets. If you position trading as the third member of your marriage/ partnership—and the one you're actually *preferring* at the moment—don't be surprised if your spouse is jealous.

Change your behaviour and your partner will change theirs, but it's up to *you* to change first.

A word of advice on new relationships and friendships

If your relationship is new, I'd be a little wary about giving away too much information about your goals and dreams with regards to the market until you're sure the relationship is going to go the distance. And be careful about sharing too much with non-trading friends.

Here are some reasons why:

- **Valuing privacy:** Your financial situation is personal and private, and you may not want to disclose it to someone you just met or don't yet know well. To be blunt, sharing such sensitive information with a new romantic partner could put you at risk of identity theft, fraud or other forms of financial exploitation.

- **Avoiding judgement:** Discussing your financial situation with a new partner or friend may lead them to form opinions or biases about you based on your financial status. This could be a problem if you're dating someone who values money and financial success above other things.

- **Establishing trust:** Trust is a crucial element in any relationship, and sharing sensitive information too soon may lead to an erosion of trust. It's important to build a strong foundation before discussing your full financial situation.

- **Focusing on other things:** In the early stages of a relationship, it's important to focus on getting to know each other and building emotional intimacy. Discussing the specifics of your finances may distract from this process and may not be the best use of your time together. However, even early in the new relationship, you can talk about your views about money and identify any potential hurdles the two of you might face.

Let's move on to a significant topic that can trip you up whether or not you happen to have a partner.

Your money scripts

I've always enjoyed all aspects of money. As a child, my prized possession was a little money box with a mechanical skeleton arm that dragged coins into a mini coffin. Oooh, I loved that thing!

I was brought up with very few material possessions and I felt acutely aware of our family's lack of money. Watching my mum go without a winter coat so her children could have warm clothes and seeing how feeding four children on a minimal budget affected her convinced me I desperately wanted my life to be different.

One day, when I was about eight years old, my grandmother said something that made things fall into place for me: 'She who has the gold, makes the rules.' I realised I wanted to make money and not be reliant on anyone else. I wanted to be the one to *make* the rules, rather than follow rules made *for* me.

I knew I wanted to be rich. Sure, as a child, I didn't know how I would get there, but I had a fire in my belly and that desire for financial stability took me to where I am today.

You can resent the rich. You can hate the few. You can be sure they got there by inheritance, deception or selling drugs. Be warned, though. This thinking guarantees you'll never amass your own fortune. You will be made safe by your thoughts. Your actions won't allow you to progress in the direction you despise. Your mind will not allow for that level of incongruity.

Money scripts are the beliefs about money that your parents and relatives unwittingly conveyed to you. They can be like the plot of a play, passed down to you and influencing your financial choices. But, just like a play, these scripts may be only partially true. The problem is, they can control your behaviour without you realising it.

Even after I started to make money, I still had some hang-ups:

- In my pantry, you'll find around 20 boxes of cereal. After eating generic home brand cardboard-tasting cereal for so many years, having yummy cereal somehow represents prosperity to me.

- I don't mind earning the money but I have an aversion to seeing how much money we're forking out on school fees and utility bills. My husband pays those accounts.

- It took me a long time to be comfortable going on an expensive holiday. It used to feel like a waste of money. I remember reading how Phil Knight (the guy behind Nike) and his wife shopped for massive amounts of toilet paper and toothpaste once their company made them into billionaires. They stocked up on 'staples' so if someone took all their money away at least they'd have plenty of these essentials. I totally understand that impulse.

What are your money hang-ups? The more aware of them you become, the less your hang-ups will have a hold over you.

The way you talk to yourself about money can dent your happiness. If you never seem to have enough, or if when you get to a certain income level you *think* you'll be happy, you may be setting yourself up for disappointment.

The Klontz Money Script Inventory identifies four common money scripts that apply to traders and investors.

Money status

Money status traders are all about the bling and showing off their wealth to impress others. People with this money script might spend more than they can afford or take risky bets in the markets or hide losses from their loved ones. They fear losing face in front of those they love. Often from a lower socioeconomic background, they may believe that if they live a virtuous life, this will lead them to impressive financial rewards. Individuals with this money script are likely to buy the flashy cars, work a 90-hour week in a high-profile job, and live in the best neighbourhoods — whether or not they can afford it.

Money worship

When you believe more money guarantees more happiness you fall victim to money worship. People who think like this may neglect their family in favour of work and always feel they don't have enough. It's common for people with lower net worth to hold these beliefs and to constantly compare themselves to others.

Author Keith Payne argues a sense of inequality can lead to impulsive and risky behaviour. The effects are similar to those brought on by a physical threat. For investors, this could mean making flashy purchases, bragging about trades or chasing high-risk, high-reward deals. FOMO (fear of missing out) is a very real threat to people in this category.

Money vigilance

Money vigilant traders feel safe when they have money but they may struggle to indulge themselves. They value hard work and saving and they don't keep financial secrets from their partners. However, their frugality may cause conflict — if, for example, their partner wants to go on a luxury trip but they lean towards a cheaper option. For a trader, being too money vigilant can mean missing out on enjoying the fruits of your labour and can lead to burnout.

Money avoidance

Money avoiders see money as a necessary evil. They believe wealth is inherently corrupting, or that they don't deserve it. Sometimes they sabotage themselves by ignoring their finances or even giving their money away. This may sound like a good deed but it may keep them from achieving their financial goals. If this sounds like you, don't let these behaviours hold you back from potential success in the markets.

Investors brought up in a religious environment may also ask themselves, 'Is it okay to be rich?'

Self-sabotage is common when their bank accounts go above a level that feels comfortable. People with these money scripts may ignore their financial statements and unconsciously want to have as little as possible.

Why it's important

Rarely will people in a relationship have identical money scripts. The odds are your partner and your friends will see the world completely differently from you, but that's the fun of it all, isn't it? The key here is to make your views explicit, so each of you can see where the other is coming from.

It's crucial to understand your own money scripts. They can have a significant impact on your investment performance.

By becoming aware of your money scripts, you gain insight into how they influence your financial decisions. Self-awareness allows you to challenge detrimental beliefs or patterns.

Money itself doesn't change who you are at your core. Rather, it amplifies your natural predispositions. If you have a genuine desire to be kind and contribute to the wellbeing of others, financial success through investing can empower you to make a more significant impact. You can support charitable causes and make a difference in the lives of those in need.

On the other hand, if you're unaware of your money scripts and act based on unconscious beliefs or fears, you may make impulsive or reckless decisions. Understanding your money scripts allows you to address any limiting beliefs, develop a healthier relationship with money, and make more informed and strategic choices.

Stop shooting yourself in the foot

According to research in the financial planning field, even some of the most diligent investors 'hesitate, fail to act, or simply do not take the agreed upon action to implement [financial] planning recommendations'. So when you become aware of your own money scripts, you're more likely to act with decisiveness and without hesitation. As I often say, good traders are action takers.

Changing your behaviour and breaking old habits is never easy. It's natural to feel resistant and to act erratically when trying to make positive changes that go against your subconscious beliefs. However, by recognising and understanding your subconscious influences, you can gain valuable insights into your behaviour and identify challenging areas of trading.

Neck deep in debt

If you're neck deep in debt, what can you do about it?

1. Find out where your money is going

The first step is to work out exactly what you have coming in and what's going out. Beware of little expenses. As Benjamin Franklin once said: 'A small leak will sink a great ship.'

Remember to include the expected as well as the unexpected costs, including:

- gifts/donations

- savings

- pets

- clothing

- accommodation

- entertainment

- food

- utilities

- insurance

- child care

- debt repayments.

Approach this fact-finding mission without judgement. Put on your private investigator's hat, and delve deep. There are some great tools to help you. I used Quicken to track everything I spent for three months, down to the dollar. Even one week of disciplined record keeping will pay dividends. There are loads of other tools available. If you need a budget, you could try Mvelopes, GoodBudget or (funnily enough) You Need a Budget. Or simply grab all your receipts and enter these into a spreadsheet, along with your statements. Getting down and dirty will enable you to work out the actual inflow and outflow of your money.

2. Think about it

Compare how much money you have coming in with how much is going out. This is easier said than done.

Look at what percentage of your total spending each financial payment represents, in comparison with your overall income. Think about whether you're comfortable with that. Consider whether it reflects your values.

3. Make some changes

If you need to make some adjustments (and you probably do, because there's always room for improvement), start looking for places to redirect spending from things you really don't care about towards the areas that mean more to you.

If your 'must have' expenses (accommodation, food, insurance, utilities, loan repayments and child care) are more than 50 per cent of your after-tax income, you are likely to struggle. It's time to downgrade the car, or your accommodation, and to examine where you can make some serious, hard-hitting changes. Think of ways you can make money by selling items you no longer use, and see whether you can switch to a higher paying job.

Yes, I'm all for making more money, but I'm also a fan of being frugal and building up your equity, even if it means making some short-term sacrifices.

If your discretionary expenses have been slashed and you're still in trouble, I'll take a stab and say your big bills are out of whack.

I recently examined the money flow of one of my traders, and I couldn't fault it. How was it that he was still in financial crisis? Well, I'll tell you. Every so often, to console himself about his life, he blew a big chunk of money on an unnecessary purchase — an antique sideboard here, an expensive guitar there — and he suffered because of it. So beware of the big periodic 'spoil yourself' purchase. Set up some circuit breakers before you buy anything over, say, $500.

If you're serious about getting out of your financial funk, follow these three steps and you'll pay down your debt, build your equity and still enjoy a few of life's comforts.

Key concepts

- Recognise the influence of your money scripts and how they shape your financial choices. Common money scripts are money status, money worship, money vigilance and money avoidance.

- Have a frank discussion with your spouse about money topics such as spending limits, financial responsibilities, acceptable spending ratios, rewards and past financial experiences.

- If you're in a new relationship, proceed with caution when discussing financial details early on. Focus on building trust and emotional intimacy before opening up about your financial situation.

- If you're neck deep in debt, take steps to understand your income and expenses, and make necessary changes to improve your financial situation. Consider making short-term sacrifices to build equity and achieve long-term financial stability.

Many people tie themselves up in knots with worry that they don't have what it takes to be a trader. One source of stress: the question of whether there's a gender gap in terms of results and methods. We'll look at this in more depth in the next chapter.

CHAPTER 11

The investment gender gap — fact or fiction?

To be a top-notch trader, you've got to prove to yourself that no matter what your inherent traits are you can conquer the markets. And when it comes to gender, there are noticeable differences in how men and women tend to invest. But is there a true winner when it comes to this battle of the sexes?

There are some things you just can't change — your age, your sex, even how supportive your partner is in relation to your aspirations. And let's not forget about your personality since it's not something you can easily swap out. These fixed traits can sometimes make you doubt whether you can really succeed as a trader. But wouldn't it be great to know if they actually hold you back?

There are noticeable differences in how men and women tend to invest, and this can affect the results they get. Let's dig deeper and see what's up.

Only 26 per cent of American women get involved with investing in the stock market, and they tend to invest less aggressively than men do. According to Gallup's 2023 estimate, 61 per cent of US adults invest in the stock market, so by inference women are poorly represented as investors. However, many studies provide evidence that female traders actually outperform their male counterparts. Despite this, according to a survey by Fidelity in 2017, only 9 per cent of women think they are better investors than men.

The markets are an equal opportunity employer and really don't care whether you're a female or a male.

This is why mindset is such an important issue to master. Perceived impediments can make a huge difference to a trader's results.

It's a concern that so many women doubt their own money management capabilities. These worries extend beyond the financial markets. According to a study conducted in March 2019 across 11 countries, researcher Jodie Gunzberg from SPGlobal discovered some pretty interesting stuff. It turns out that in both the US and Canada, fewer women feel they're in 'excellent' or 'good' financial shape compared to men.

And here's another eye-opener: if they were hit with a financial setback, like losing their job, 22 per cent of North American women say they wouldn't be able to afford their current lifestyle right away. That's almost double the percentage of American men (13 per cent).

It's a catch 22 situation for women — they see the potential for financial gain in the markets, but they often don't have the same level of financial security to take the risks that come with investing. Because women perceive themselves to be in a more precarious position with their finances, this increases their reluctance towards taking on a supposedly risky investment in the stock market.

Testosterone and other hormones

The way our brains are wired can have a significant impact on our performance as traders, and there are noticeable differences between male and female brains. From birth, physiological variances between the sexes are apparent. Whether this is the effect of nature or nurture, understanding these differences is crucial in assessing how they can either enhance or hinder your investment abilities.

Let's zoom in on the role of hormones, particularly testosterone. Professor James Dabbs from Georgia State University conducted a study that measured testosterone levels in males across various fields. His findings revealed that those who excelled in their respective endeavours had higher testosterone levels than those who achieved less. Interestingly, the thrill of accomplishing something also triggered an increase in testosterone production. It's worth noting, of course, that heightened testosterone levels have also been linked to aggression.

Based on these discoveries, it's reasonable to assume high-achieving males in the trading field are likely to have elevated testosterone levels. However, the study suggests that in order to maintain positive outcomes, these high achievers need to find ways to mitigate the influence of testosterone on their behaviour. If those traders can calm down quickly after a testosterone spike, they are more likely to trade profitably. Emotional regulation is the key.

In other words, higher testosterone levels don't necessarily make men better traders; as we've noted, studies suggest women often achieve better returns.

Research indicates women often struggle to set aside their problems and frequently benefit from discussing situations with others to find solutions. Female traders may have a greater need to share their wins and losses with a friend or confidant. By acknowledging these needs, each gender can navigate the investment journey more smoothly.

Confidence in decisions

Analysing the data from a US brokerage firm, researchers Barber and Odean found that men traded 45 per cent more but earned 1.4 per cent less annually. This gender gap was even wider among single traders, with men trading 67 per cent more and earning 2.3 per cent less. The researchers attribute these results mainly to the detrimental effects of overconfidence and excessive trading.

A study by Fidelity Investments involved a demographically representative sample of 2995 adults in the US and replicated the finding that women outperformed men. According to Fidelity client data, women, on average, outperformed men by 40 basis points, or 0.4 per cent. This difference may seem small, but the impact over time is significant.

'The good news is many women are putting themselves in the financial driver's seat, taking positive steps to save and invest effectively for their future', said Kathleen Murphy, president of personal investing at Fidelity. However, there is still work to be done and saving alone is not enough to keep pace with inflation. So, unless you're investing then you're likely losing money.

Murphy goes on to say that it is then critical to take the next step and 'ensure that savings are invested properly and generating growth' in order to help women 'progress toward their financial goals and live the lives they deserve.'

One of the biggest needs for me and my women friends is that we need to feel safe. It's important we have this need met and reinforced before we experience the freedom to follow a trading plan.

For women, feeling safe financially and emotionally is more multi-layered than most of us realise. Past investments and money scripts can rock female traders in many ways. Knowledge is power, so educating yourself about the markets can really help.

Portfolio turnover

According to studies conducted by Barber and Odean, there is a clear correlation between portfolio turnover and ultimate performance. When a portfolio has an annual turnover rate exceeding 200 per cent, the average annual net return lags behind the market index by 10.3 per cent. In a study involving 78 000 households, it was observed women had an annual portfolio turnover of approximately 53 per cent, while men had a turnover of 77 per cent.

The research suggests that women exhibit confidence in their abilities when provided with unambiguous and immediate feedback. However, in situations where feedback is absent or ambiguous, women are less confident and often underestimate their investing performance compared to men.

Given that feedback in the financial markets is often ambiguous, women may be more inclined to wait for optimal opportunities before making investments. This cautious approach could explain both their lower trading levels compared to those of men, and their higher levels of success.

Activity isn't the same as profitability

It's easy to see why 'action'-related metaphors about the markets are so seductive. And if you've bought into the idea that the stock market is all glam and excitement, your view of what it really takes to trade smart will be clouded.

It requires the ability to sit with positions over time, and to tolerate repetitive tasks.

The famous trader Jesse Livermore said, 'It never was my thinking that made the big money for me. It always was my sitting. Got that? My sitting tight!'

Many traders enter the markets with the misconception that effective investing involves a roller-coaster ride of dramatic emotions, being in the market at all times, and trading frequently and aggressively.

Interestingly, research has found most tellingly being 'in the action' is more important than being profitable for the vast majority of traders. *Activity* is often more important to the trader than the *consequences* of that activity. Some traders enjoy the entertainment value of the markets so much they fail to focus on profitability.

*Regardless of gender, sometimes the best action you can take is to **pause** before you take the next step. Traders often need to take a beat, to sharpen their axe rather than plunge forward without thinking about the consequences.*

Female-managed funds outperform

The evidence suggests there are differences between females and males in terms of their risk appetite and asset management strategies, particularly during downturns. Numerous studies demonstrate that businesses controlled by women tend to outperform those controlled by men.

In early 2017, journalist Jan Wieczner reported in *Fortune* that women-managed hedge funds outperformed the industry, returning 3.65 per cent compared to the industry's 2.23 per cent.

Also, when examining the performance of investment portfolios during the market drawdown in 2022, assets managed by women performed better than those managed by their male counterparts. This analysis considered returns from 80 investment portfolios across 73 asset managers.

Interestingly, evidence published in *Institutional Investor* magazine suggests in times of stress female fund managers take fewer risks than male fund managers, yet they achieve the same performance. Women tend to be more conservative and play it safe during periods of negative market sentiment. They take fewer risks but earn the same as men, which is ideal because risk minimisation is the key to longevity in the investing game.

The same study found that male money managers took on 'significantly more' total fund risk when sentiment was bad. This risk appetite did not derive commensurate positive rewards. 'We find no significant relation between the higher risk due to bad sentiment and performance. Hence, fund investors do not receive a compensation for the higher risk that (male) managers take on,' the authors reported.

Embrace your potential

It's crucial to recognise that the data strongly supports women's potential for investing success. Women have every reason to believe in their ability to thrive in the trading arena. Despite the perception that investing is predominantly a male-dominated domain, numerous studies consistently demonstrate that women outperform their male counterparts.

In fact, women tend to excel in almost every measure of effectiveness, including actual performance, risk evaluation and portfolio management.

As a female investor, even if you occasionally experience self-doubt, don't let your gender become a barrier to exploring investing as a profession or a source of income. Engaging in financial markets can provide an opportunity for you to leverage your calmness, humility and meticulous preparation before entering new positions.

Seek support from fellow investors and find trusted individuals so you can discuss your decisions and seek valuable insights. Additionally, remember to prioritise downtime and self-care to ensure you can effectively manage the cognitive demands of investing. Embrace your rightful place as an investor, trust in your abilities, and leverage the data that consistently shows women's success in this field.

And remember, regardless of gender, trading requires a high-performance mindset, and acknowledging the need for recovery is essential.

Key concepts

- Investing gender differences do exist, but they do not determine success. Women often underestimate their abilities and face unique challenges related to financial security, but they have been shown to outperform men in investment returns.

- Confidence in investment decisions differs between the sexes, with men often exhibiting overconfidence and excessive trading. Women tend to be more cautious and patient, leading to higher levels of success.

- Portfolio turnover and activity do not necessarily correlate with profitability. Taking time to pause, analyse and make informed decisions is often more effective than constant action.

- Women tend to excel in risk evaluation and portfolio management, and female-controlled businesses consistently demonstrate strong performance in the financial industry.

Have you ever wished you had had a money mentor in your childhood? In the next chapter, we'll explore how you can become that mentor and make a difference in the next generation's financial success.

Raising money-wise kids to shape the financial confidence of the next generation

Experienced traders often say they wish they had been taught the secrets of successful investing when they were young. Many had to learn through a series of tough experiences. This chapter explores how you can involve your children in your trading life, setting them up for long-term financial success.

Recent studies indicate parents engage in fewer distinct conversations about money with their daughters than with their sons. This may contribute to lower confidence levels among adult women when it comes to investments.

Through interviews conducted with over 100 school-aged children, averaging 10 years of age, it was revealed that parents exhibit gender-based distinctions in the topics they discuss regarding money with their children. Parents talk to their girls about family finances, spending money, earning and checking the balance of their bank accounts. Boys are more likely to be taught by their parents about saving up for particular assets, borrowing and budgeting. Researcher Lynsey Romo observes, 'I think parents might just have this latent view that boys are more of the providers.' She goes on to comment, 'There might be some latent cultural assumptions there, for sure.'

But what can we do?

Here are three specific methods you can use to help your children develop a wealth mindset.

1. Become aware of how you're talking to children about investing

Consider the impact of what they take in subconsciously.

As you sat at the top of the stairs as a child, what did you hear your parents talk about? This hits just as hard as the obvious things your folks did to teach you about money.

When children ask for something, parents often say, 'We can't afford it,' reinforcing scarcity thinking. Instead, try saying, 'I choose not to spend my money on that.'

Become aware of your own money scripts implanted from the time you were a child. That way you'll be less likely to pass on any of your dubious thinking about money to your children.

After making a large trading mistake, psychologist Brad Klontz said, 'When I put it in the context of these financial flash points that went back for generations in my family system, it actually freed me up a bit to give myself a break and be like, "Okay, great. I made this mistake. I get why I did it. Now, what can I do about it?"'

2. Talk about money openly

Discover what your kids know about investing and their future goals. Discuss their long-term, medium-term and short-term goals and link these to age-appropriate actions with their pocket money.

3. Start when they're young

Involve your children in your investing activities, and you might discover an unexpected advantage. Many of us over-complicate our investing strategies. Consider asking your child to be a sounding board and explain your trading system in straightforward terms. Simplifying it to a level under-standable by a child can enhance your methods. Taking time to engage with your child and articulate your goals will yield multiple benefits.

A warning

As Ross Campbell highlights in his book *How to Really Love Your Child*, one of the fundamental needs of children, regardless of age, is meaningful eye contact. While I understand that investing can be captivating, it's important to exercise caution. If you constantly focus on your computer and rarely give your child your undivided attention, they may resent your involvement in the stock market.

Sometimes it may appear as though your child is intentionally interrupting your analysis time, but from their perspective trading is, in a way, diverting your attention away from them.

Most people agree that one of the primary responsibilities of parents is to inspire their children to discover their own solutions to life's challenges. By strategically introducing your child to the world of trading and investing early, you can set them on a path towards future financial independence.

Get your children involved in your trader's life, and they'll reap the rewards for decades.

Key concepts

- Early education matters. Teach your children how to invest early in order to set them up for long-term financial success.

- Break gender stereotypes. Challenge gender distinctions in money conversations to boost confidence and empower girls in investing.

- Open communication. Talk openly about money, understand your kids' goals and involve them in trading activities while keeping things simple.

Maintaining connections with others is a crucial aspect of being human. Yet an imbalance in income can strain friendships. In the next chapter we'll talk about how to prevent investing from negatively affecting your relationships with your friends.

CHAPTER 13

How to stop money ripping apart friendships

Connection with others is essential, but when there's a financial gap, friendships can suffer. Let's explore what to look out for and how to prevent investing from creating a rift between mates.

In my corporate role I was 100 per cent sure hard work was the key. I slugged it out, working 8-, then 10-, then 12-hour days. I said no to friends who wanted to meet me for dinner. But without attention, unappreciated relationships slink away into the night.

Far too often I said yes to my boss but no to my friends and family, who wanted to see more of me. To make choices like this is to risk losing the true friends who will sustain us in later life.

When you're a child it's easy to make friends. You're put in the same class, you're roughly the same age and activities such as sport split you up into smaller interest groups. You spend a solid eight hours a day together playing, learning and just goofing off.

As we get older, the chances of these magical 'friendship years' being recreated begin to recede. By the time you've run around after your own family, earned a living and tried to carve out some little chunk of time to pursue the things that are important to you, you don't have much energy left for your friends. But something far more insidious gets in the way of your adult friendships: that's when there's a big difference in earnings.

The green-eyed monster is always present, so whether you're hanging out with more successful investors or you're a star performer yourself, you'll need to consider it.

As a beginner trader, know that a dream is at its most fragile when it is first birthed. So be careful about confiding in your friends until you're sure you've committed to your dreams.

As you become a more experienced trader, barbs or negative comments won't affect you as much.

The fact is, you won't feel ready when you're starting. Point to *one* successful trader who hasn't an attitude of 'I've got this!' (before they really have got it). Point to one who was fully and completely ready and knew everything about trading before they put a dollar in the markets. I'll bet you can't. That's why you have to protect your mindset, especially when you're starting.

The actor Hugh Laurie observed, 'It's a terrible thing, I think, in life to wait until you're ready. I have this feeling now that actually no one is ever ready to do anything. There is almost no such thing as ready. There is only *now.*'

When I look back over all the major decisions in my life and think about how I 'felt' before leaping, I realise I never felt ready. I just leapt.

What if you are right now as close to being ready as you'll ever be?

What if, when you look back on your life, your biggest regret was that you wasted so much time waiting? Waiting to find the space to learn, waiting to be better?

My friend, this is it.

This is your life, right here, right now.

Today is the day.

Every day is the day.

Life waits for no one. So if you let your friends talk you out of becoming an investor, that's a crying shame.

Here's how to maintain friendships when your friends' money scripts are different from yours.

1. Look, listen and learn

Pay attention to subtle cues that suggest your friend is in a different financial situation. If you're the one struggling, remind yourself that your friend's dilemmas are important to them even if they're outside your realm of concern. Whether to holiday in Hawaii or Tahiti could be of key importance to the happiness of their family, so before you scoff, take this into account. And be aware that while we may have access to the entire film of our own lives, usually we see only the extracted highlights of the lives of our friends, especially on social media.

If you're the one with more money, remember it's obnoxious to rub people's noses in it. Financial good fortune is not a surrogate for good character. You must earn your friends' respect the same way you earned your money—through focused attention.

2. Make expectations explicit

Don't wait until the end of the evening to discuss splitting the bill. Ask for separate bills or before you order the lobster say, 'Let's just cover our own expenses tonight,' to alleviate any anxiety experienced by the one with less cash. If the cash-challenged person keeps wondering about how they're going to cover your swish dish choice all night, they really won't be relaxed enough to enjoy the evening. Yet if you feel that you have to order the least expensive dish on the menu to keep your friend happy, that will deplete your enjoyment.

And be careful where you end up holidaying if you're travelling with friends whose incomes are different. Little things can grate. Want to go on a vacation together? Don't pretend you're okay sharing a room if you're not.

If your wallet is full and you want to shout your financially challenged friend, try framing it around an event. If you can't treat your friends now and again, it certainly takes the fun out of having an extra stash of money. If you're on the receiving end, simply show gratitude by saying 'thanks' — and sit back and enjoy.

3. Make it less taboo

Let's face it, it can be tough to talk about money. Make the first move. Start a conversation about your money scripts. Maybe your struggling actor friend can show you how to be more frugal. Perhaps your market wizard mate can help you plan out how much you'll need to retire in style. That's what friends do. They challenge each other by providing another perspective, and they stick by each other, even when their money scripts are different.

By opening up about money and talking about it with your friends, you're more likely to develop your common interests. You never know, maybe your friend actually has an interest in investing they've never mentioned. It'd be good to find out, hey?

Be aware, however, that your own desire to move forward just may mean leaving someone behind.

Imagine this. You've made the decision to leap. You're gonna do it! You're finally going to become the trader you know you're capable of being. Choirs are singing, birds are tweeting... the whole world lights up as you get ready to step into the bright daylight of trading. BUT what if someone you love doesn't feel the same way? What if they say something hurtful to you about your decision? It's more common than you'd think.

Your imminent success can trigger feelings of inadequacy and jealousy in others. Things like this trigger fears of disconnection and shake everyone up.

So first, who are these people who possibly don't want the best for you or might feel jealous? Are those you really love, trust and care for feeling threatened by your potential success? What's behind their impulse to squash your dreams? Could it be possible they're just trying to keep you safe? Maybe you're rocking the boat and making them feel inadequate?

Sometimes motives are not obvious.

You may have to put some thought into broaching the topic. Your conversation might go something like this: 'I want to chat with you about my new career as a trader. I want to rely on you for your love, support and compassion. Investing effectively is really important to me, and *you* are very important to me. Can I ask you what you really feel, because I'm sensing you don't believe in me.'

Then, if it becomes clear you're not going to be able to move forward with them on this topic, you may need to say, 'I hear you, and I appreciate your concern, but this is what I mean to do. If we can't agree on it, let's drop the subject. Say what you want to say now, but after today I'd prefer not to discuss it again.'

To do this, in the right tone and with the right level of care and love, you must really *want* to achieve your goal of being an exceptional trader.

State what you need from your friend. If they cannot provide it, drop the subject.

Stand your ground. Don't let the views of others drag you down.

Weird things people have said to me

'Do you really think you can be a full-time trader? I don't think it's something any woman has done before.'

'You realise you're making a fool of yourself by writing a book?'

'Your husband will start to feel inadequate if you earn more money than he does.'

'You won't have enough money to live well in old age.'

I find it curious that people want to steal someone else's dreams and hopes for the future. I've never understood this, and never will.

I continue to pursue my goals anyway. That's my act of rebellion in the face of a world that tells me the way I earn money and the lifestyle I've chosen aren't good enough.

Judgement from others

Sometimes you'll hear the most irritating comments about the trader's life you've chosen. Here are some more of the stupid things people have said to me:

'Options trading … that will never work.' — my uncle

'It's great you wrote a book about options. I always believed in you.' — the same uncle

'So you want to be a trader. Just as well you've got a nice husband to support you.' — my dad over Sunday lunch

'If you're having trouble affording a house, I could lend you the deposit.' — my brother-in-law, who didn't know I'd chosen to rent while I built up my investment equity

'You're a woman, you'll never make it as a trader. It's an old-boys club.' — Richard Pratt (yes, that Richard Pratt)

'You'll never make a full-time income out of investing.' — my former accountant (I dumped him after I made more in a year out of the markets than I guessed he was making as a salary.)

'Trading? That's like gambling.' — more people have said this over the past three decades than I can remember

'I wish you'd grow some breasts to give me something to look at in your videos other than your huge clown mouth.' — an articulate, succinct reader of my free newsletter.

If someone has given you some lip, take it as evidence you may be doing the right thing.

Some comebacks

The newscaster David Brinkley declared, 'A successful man is one who can lay a firm foundation with the bricks others have thrown at him.'

It's good to have the support of other traders when the misjudgements of others, especially of those you love, threaten to drain you. Here are some comebacks you can use if a friend makes an inaccurate statement about trading:

- 'What makes you say that?'

- 'You realise this is more than "just a hobby" to me, don't you? I'd like your support but I'm going to do this with or without you.'

- 'We'll see if you feel that way when the money rolls in.' Say this enigmatically before turning on your heel and walking out of the room. (Don't trip.)

- 'I used to think that too, until I met lots of people who have replaced their incomes through trading.'

In the end, you'll only receive what you continue to tolerate. The stronger you are, the more the people around you will fall into line. If you waver and falter in your commitment to your future, the jackals will sense your weakness and go for your jugular.

But if you've tried to explain to no avail, you're within your rights to say, 'I've heard what you have to say, and I'm not prepared to listen any more. If you can't support me, please keep your views to yourself.' (You may need to say this a few times, but eventually you'll have to put your foot down.)

If you have a vision for your family, don't you dare give up. Find people who believe in you. Continue to strive or your future will be mediocre and unfulfilling.

I will fight anyone who tries to take away this right — I will fight for me but also for you.

Probably even more for you.

When I'm defending *your* right to be a trader, my voice is stronger, less hesitant. Borrow my strength and we'll stand together, shoulder to shoulder. Not leaning on each other but strengthening each other.

Even if you disagree with your loved one's decisions and choices, pure, real, unconditional love is wanting the best for them. It might be a good time to remind the people giving you a hard time of this definition around about now.

Societal expectations stuff us to the brim, until suddenly we're too heavy to move. Protect your heart from the disparaging remarks of those who truly don't have your best interests in mind.

Quite simply, 'they' will always be surprised by the 'you' who achieves.

And 'they' don't deserve your attention.

Revel in your choice to be a trader.

Defend it against people who don't share your vision.

Key concepts

- Nurture friendships even if you have financial differences. Recognise the impact of earning disparities. Pay attention to subtle cues and empathise with your friends' financial concerns.

- Pursue your goals. Address the concerns of friends and loved ones through open and honest communication. Stand your ground and assert your commitment to your chosen path.

We often ignore the importance of recovery strategies. Elite athletes don't just run themselves into the ground. They build in strategic pauses to renew their strength. You're about to learn the latest science-based, evidence-backed methods that will enable you to keep charging towards your goals.

KEY 4

Recharge and renew

Stay energised for optimal performance

Years ago I remember an argument I had with my husband. 'I'll be back late tonight,' I called through my car window on my way to work — when I had 'a real job'.

'Later than last night?' he bristled. 'I get the feeling you're saving your best "you" for the office.'

Oooh… that stung.

But he was right. Painful truths can land with a thud.

Back then I was spending 80 hours a week trying to impress people I didn't respect to win the next promotion. Leaving home when it was dark and getting back after dark. What in the hell was I doing?

Corporate life can suck you dry. By giving your all, every day, you can find you have very little left over for your family. You can end up depleted beyond the point where you can look after yourself adequately, and that can lead to you feeling resentful or, worse, struggling with health issues.

Thank goodness I learned how to trade. Now my family gets the best of me. As the breadwinner, I call the shots and determine how many hours I work. I get to be a full-time mum. And my husband is a full-time dad.

Some great traders are workaholics, putting in long hours and thinking about the markets 24/7. The big risk is they'll eventually fry their brains and hit a wall, leading to financial losses, failed relationships and health issues. No, thank you!

Many traders march to the steady drumbeat of burnout. They proudly identify as an A-Type personality and they pile activity on activity without taking time to stop, look, listen and live. Success isn't worth much if you can't enjoy it.

On the other hand, there are those who can't seem to get started because they prioritise playtime over work.

The perfect balance means working hard and playing hard, finding joy in the whole process. You can't wait for your fun days off and you're excited to get back to the markets when the time is right. It's a state of functional bliss very few ever reach, but you can achieve it if you decide that's what you want and you make a plan for how to get there.

This is one of the keys to effective trading. You can find balance, and I'm about to show you exactly how…

CHAPTER 14

Avoid trader burnout

The pendulum swings perpetually between busyness and the need for downtime. Finding the right balance will help you make better investment decisions and go the distance.

One morning last January I woke up with absolutely nothing to do. No deadlines, no podcasts to make, no trades to put onto the markets, no emails to answer. Life was suddenly quiet... too quiet. I felt my heart rate increase, and I started to have a mini-freakout.

Arthur Schopenhauer's words resonate here: 'Life swings like a pendulum backward and forward between pain and boredom.' We're either racing at full speed or coming to a screeching halt, rarely enjoying the gentle swaying between busyness and relaxation.'

Have you ever felt like you're constantly searching for the next big thing, always on the go and never taking a break?

In his book *Curious Habits*, Luke Mathers suggests a reason why. 'When we experience a gradual narrowing of things that bring us joy—we only feel good when we're striving for something new. But this can leave us feeling overloaded and burnt out.'

It's important to give yourself permission to reset and take a break. Take a week off, download a good book and chill out. Once you allow yourself to do it, resetting becomes a piece of cake. Hunker down before you spring up again.

Of course success isn't just about piling up cash. Ask anyone who has worked themselves into a health crisis. They'll tell you they'd swap every cent in their account to get back to their prime. I don't have a problem with the standard-issue workaholic who is occasionally overwhelmed by over-scheduling. What I'm talking about is the *habitually* busy person, burning the midnight oil for weeks, months or even years, missing the children's football matches, unable to remember their last day off.

I understand, you're trying to juggle investing, running a business, a job, a life … and that will sometimes play havoc with anyone's schedule. But the pendulum must swing back to a more moderate pace between the frantic moments.

Usually I don't see those 'moderate' traders, though. Because by the time they turn to me they're already a basket case, desperate and at the end of their tether, tackling crisis after crisis with ferocious regularity. And there's the irony. All that relentless martyrdom isn't necessarily rewarded in the real world. Your brain is thrashed, your energy supply drained, your creativity dried up, and your mojo jumped out the window long ago.

All because you lost sight of what matters most in your life.

Four stages of burnout

There are usually four stages people move through when experiencing burnout:

1. physical, mental and emotional exhaustion

2. shame and doubt, turning inwards

3. cynicism and callousness, turning outwards

4. failure, helplessness and crisis.

The further along you are in this process, the more you need to focus on your recovery and learning about how you can make some changes in your life. If you're in stages 1 to 3 you can recognise this, and you'll very likely be able to recover using the specific techniques we discuss in this book. Around stage 4 there is a tipping point, where you may need to seek professional help.

Burnout is one of the biggest challenges short-term traders face. The need to make fast decisions, with significant consequences and the impact on your identity, produces a pressure-cooker situation.

A couple of times in my life I've been burned out so badly that I was drained of all happiness. In that state even a baby's laugh couldn't move me. When I left my corporate job to become a full-time trader I encountered a huge health issue. I had been promoted to a level where I was flying from city to city all the time. I could never keep up with the work and I didn't see any progress. I felt like the hamster who could never run fast enough on the spinning wheel. It sapped my energy and made me forget to be grateful for the things that were going well in my life.

Day traders sometimes end up feeling this way because everything is happening in such a compressed time frame, which is why their burnout rate is so high.

Most people today have two modes: fast as hell and collapsed. If they're the only two states you know, you're not being productive and happiness will be elusive. If you're on the brink of burning out, recognise it and pull back. Not only will you live to trade another day, you'll enjoy it all so much more too.

Renowned psychologist Hendrie Weisinger, author of *Performing Under Pressure: The science of doing your best when it matters most*, emphasises the distinction between stress and pressure. Understanding the difference allows you to implement the most appropriate strategies for recovery.

Stress

Stress occurs when you face overwhelming demands but lack the resources to meet them. These resources can include time, money or energy. It's the feeling of being overloaded and overwhelmed, facing looming deadlines without the hours, funds or stamina to cope with them.

Unfortunately, some traders must go through a crisis to finally get their own attention and make an effort to improve their system. Psychologists call this *one-trial learning*. The one experience is so devastating that it forces a change in behaviour — painful but effective. A quick whack to the side of the head can sometimes be the best thing to ever happen to you, as long as your head isn't completely knocked off in the process! But unless you can experience the pain of loss and analyse where you need to improve — put on your crash helmet when you next feel the urge to trade.

The problem with this type of acute pain is that it may put you off trading altogether. Sometimes things can just become too much to bear, and it seems simpler to reject the whole practice rather than attempt it again. This type of reaction must be avoided at all costs.

Stress can be alleviated either by increasing your available resources or by reducing the demands placed upon you. It is influenced by how you *perceive* the pressures you face. Neurologically, stress hormones are released to heighten your alertness and focus on the task at hand. Cortisol and adrenaline are released to prepare you for action and to confront the perceived threat. They can trigger a range of responses, including fighting, fleeing or freezing.

Beginning their investing education and starting to trade can generate a bucketload of stress in some people. There's just so much to do they're quickly overwhelmed.

When I get overwhelmed I tend to shut down.
I can't take in any more information so the forward
momentum I was starting to experience grinds
to a halt.

Your fight, flight or freeze response takes over. Your primitive monkey brain sees the threat and screams, 'Run away! No, stand your ground and fight! Arrgh — crap yourself and hide! Bite something!'

To this part of your mind, every threat has a beginning but no end. And *every* threat could kill you.

These primal responses may help you survive a life-or-death confrontation with a tiger, but let's face it, they are fairly useless when it comes to responding to a threatening or confusing financial market. Clearly, however, you need to learn how to manage your emotions, because they can impact more than your investing results.

Nurture yourself

Here's a challenge for you. For today—just today—think of yourself as a toddler. If you had a three-year-old you were responsible for, you'd play nice, fun music for them. You'd make sure they had a little nap when they needed it and got to bed on time and that they played with friends who made them laugh. You'd pull out the paints, and finger paint with them, or do something else that fed their creative soul. You wouldn't let your precious darling eat too much sugar or watch too much TV. You'd protect their body as well as their mind.

For today, why don't you do this *for you*? If you're uncomfortable, change into something soft and comfortable that allows you to move freely. Protect your sleep time. Eat to restore your energy. Hang out with people who make you laugh.

Care for your inner toddler. Nurture yourself.

Do that at least once a month. You'll get your energy back and your creativity will surprise you. Oh yeah... plus, I guarantee there will be another hidden benefit. You'll see patterns, and connections in the markets, learn trading principles with remarkable ease and develop new ways of thinking. Worth giving it a shot, don't you think?

Perception

Kelly McGonigal, a health psychologist at Stanford University, presents a fascinating perspective on stress. Like many other researchers, her primary aim was to help people avoid stress. However, her research results flipped her initial expectations on their head.

She found that, contrary to popular belief, in certain circumstances stress can have a positive effect on your health. The small cohort of Americans who viewed stress positively had a 43 per cent lower chance of premature death compared to those who saw stress as destructive. McGonigal found when individuals learn how to think of stress as a challenge, rather than a threat, it could stimulate growth. What gives you butterflies also lights you up. And it can be traced right back to the neurotransmitter level.

Reframing your feelings of nervousness as feelings of *excitement* can lead to several benefits. Embracing stress increases resilience. When we accept and even welcome stress, we can enhance our cardiovascular health, foster meaningful social connections and even live longer.

By facing and overcoming challenges, we develop the ability to bounce back stronger and more resilient than before.

If the stress is too great or lasts too long, though, the body will fail to adapt. Hans Selye calls this the 'exhaustion stage'. Rather than prompting growth, chronic stress is more likely to lead to elevated inflammation.

When we're under pressure that we perceive negatively, something in us snaps and we become paranoid, assuming the worst. It crushes our sense of fun and our passion. I see this in my own life when I'm not coping, and I see it in my friends. People can become the worst version of themselves ... or the best.

Some take it as a springboard to launch themselves into their true life's purpose. Recognising what they *don't* want makes what they *do* want become clearer. Like an old-fashioned camera struggling to focus, suddenly all the fuzzy edges sharpen. Confusion falls away, revealing a clear path forward.

We can allow stress to crush us... or we can use it to push against. It's our choice.

Pressure

Pressure, as defined by Weisinger, is created by the demands placed on you by your environment. It is possible to be in a pressure-oriented environment without feeling stressed, because how you react to that pressure is a matter of choice.

Figuring out whether you're dealing with stress or just feeling the pressure can help you choose the right steps to protect your mental wellbeing. When experiencing stress, there are several options available to you. You can shift your perception of a situation — say, by going for a walk, engaging in a conversation with a friend or practising yoga. By either reducing the load, recognising the load is temporary or adjusting your attitude, you can effectively manage your stressful circumstances.

Under pressure, you can modify your environment. For instance, you can organise your trading desk to minimise distractions and establish routines that help you focus.

Living in a high-pressure environment can mean you're more likely to overreact to even small things. Everyday activities can feel like matters of life and death when our environment is not conducive to success.

Dr John Tickell, author of *Laughter, Sex, Vegetables and Fish*, observes, 'Pressure is incredible stuff. It is both frightening and exciting. In short bursts it is stimulating. In long, drawn-out doses, it is soul-destroying'. He distinguishes the difference between stress and pressure like this: 'Pressure is out there. Stress is in here.' He explains that stress doesn't need to make us sick and deplete us. If we adopt the right framing and the right habits, it can invigorate us.

The STUFF framework

Using a framework to identify when you might be susceptible to the negative effects of pressure can be helpful. Dr Steven Jones has introduced a useful acronym to assess such situations — STUFF, which stands for:

Stress

Timeframe

Uncertainty

Fear

Fatigue.

When you feel pressured, it's often because you are dealing with a project or situation that encompasses these characteristics. Trading has a significant amount of STUFF woven into it.

That's why it's crucial to prioritise and maintain effective recovery habits. By taking care of yourself and implementing strategies to address the challenges posed by stress, timeframe, uncertainty, fear and fatigue, you can navigate the trading environment more effectively.

Poor sleep patterns, diet or exercise habits may individually have only a small impact on your investment performance. Cumulatively, however, neglecting them can significantly hinder your chances of success.

Key concepts

- Carve out time in your schedule to unwind, think deeply and recover. Change your perception so you enjoy the upside of performing with excitement, rather than the downside of being crushed by pressure.

- Sustaining high performance requires intentional effort. Distinguishing between stress and pressure can help prevent burnout and provide options for resolving challenging situations. By pre-planning how you will respond to the pressures of being a trader, you increase your likelihood of excelling.

- The skills you develop come from struggle. Growth happens when you adapt to the stressor. By experiencing mild stress, or more significant stress while allowing yourself enough rest to assimilate the lessons, you become stronger.

Had some knocks in the markets? It's surprising how much this can impact you both emotionally and physically. You need to learn how to bounce back when the market has pushed you off balance. Keep reading so you can learn how to master this skill.

CHAPTER 15

Recover from the market knocks — fast!

To be an effective trader you need to be able to bounce back from sudden market shocks. Learning the best ways to recover will keep you performing at the top of your game.

I was chatting with a trader the other day, listening to how she had just faced the worst investing loss of her life. She described how much she had lost and, honestly, it was truly hideous! The sad part was that I remember her telling me the same story around 18 months ago.

I asked, in as empathic a voice as I could muster, 'Do you remember the hit you took last time? Didn't you learn from that, to make sure you never went through that sort of pain again?'

She replied, 'I had to work hard to forgive myself for that loss so I could move on. Now I'll have to try and forgive myself for *this* loss.'

Hmm... This exchange got me thinking. Is self-forgiveness a useful trait? What happens when people forgive themselves but don't learn the lessons inherent in the slap they've received? Are they destined to repeat the same painful experience again and again?

Most of our life is spent trying to maximise pleasure and avoid pain, so you might not like what you are about to read in this chapter. Popular psychology feeds into this human instinct: again and again we are told to forgive ourselves unequivocally. Many people believe memories are held at a cellular level, and unless you cleanse yourself of the bad experience, you're actually storing this negative experience, which will manifest in poor health. Perhaps this is true. Perhaps not. I can guarantee, though, that unless you allow yourself to feel the pain of a loss and to fully feel the devastation and humiliation of your poor decisions, you will be destined to repeat your mistakes. Glossing over the experience, and trying to go straight from the experience to forgiveness, instead of fully undergoing the pain, is totally counterproductive.

We pass through a range of emotions when we experience a loss in the market. First shock and anger, and once we have moved through this raw emotion phase we are likely to look for ways to reject the experience and find excuses for our part in the loss. Passing through the acute phase of pain is necessary. It makes us less inclined to repeat the experience. If we are to mature as investors, we must accept this experience before moving on. This progression is neatly captured in the acronym *Sara*:

Shock

Anger

Rejection

Acceptance.

The problems arise when people move directly from the initial shock phase to trying to accept the experience and forgiving themselves, in an effort to avoid the pain of anger and self-recrimination.

You are allowed to feel negative emotions! In these days of sugar-coating, making the best of every experience and positive self-talk, we seem to have forgotten the power of pain and the constructive role it plays in our lives. If you have made a big loss, or contributed to your own demise in any way, you should be angry at yourself. Try to avoid this pain and you will be destined to repeat your mistakes and you'll be unlikely to trade effectively in the future.

Some people are less combustible than others, and won't need to sink into the depths of self-despair before they can move on to greatness. But all of us at some stage have made a trading mistake, and if we forgive ourselves too readily we will miss the lesson inherent in the experience.

Discipline yourself or the markets will discipline you. I know which I would prefer.

Most loss of wealth comes from carelessness. When you stray from your trading plan, or don't even follow one, money dissolves.

Most wealth creation comes from calculated effort. The $100 note you're holding will only multiply to become $1000 if you respect it. Don't let small amounts of money slip through your fingers. Treat it with respect and it will grow. Don't fritter it away.

A few years ago I provided seed capital for a friend's startup. He took the $250 000 I invested... and spent it on travel and sex workers. Oh yes, that's exactly what happened. He posted the pictures on Facebook to prove it.

I can laugh about that experience now... sort of. The saying 'Tragedy plus time equals comedy' seems especially fitting.

When you've made a mistake with money, the lessons you'll learn are invaluable. For example, now when a friend asks me to invest in their venture, I examine it even more carefully than if a stranger had pitched an investment. There's a greater level of risk, after all. If the friend's venture doesn't work out, there's a possibility you'll lose not only your capital but the friendship as well.

This game can feel like an endless grind, especially when you've been at it for a while. It's repetitive and demands unwavering focus over extended periods to achieve success. And as if that isn't enough, the markets can blindside you with unexpected shocks along the way. Whether it's a monumental win or a devastating loss, learning to bounce back is essential.

The good news is that overcoming these challenges is where true growth and resilience are forged. The thicker the skin, the fuller the wallet. With perseverance and the ability to recover from setbacks, you can navigate the unpredictable waters of investing and find success in the face of adversity.

Jesse Livermore's advice in *How to Trade in Stocks*, written in 1940, continues to resonate with traders today: 'Keep stress at bay — act in all ways to keep the mind clear and your judgement correct. I did all I could to achieve this in my physical life by going to bed early, eating and drinking lightly, taking exercise, standing upright at the stock ticker, standing while on the telephone and demanding silence in the office.'

Now we have the ability to track our physiology scientifically, the research strongly backs Jesse's thoughts on the importance of self-care to achieving optimal performance.

Little things can make a big difference to your investing success. Your sleeping patterns, your diet and your exercise routine — they may seem unrelated, but they all contribute, even if perhaps only marginally, to your overall trading performance. Of course, there are significant, more direct ways you can move the needle, such as following your plan diligently, setting those crucial stop-loss orders for each trade and using appropriate position sizing. However, when you're looking at skilled performance at an elite level, those extra 1 per cent advantages can make all the difference. Individually, they may seem insignificant, but together they can carry you over the line to success.

Manage your energy

Athletes put huge amounts of effort into managing their personal energy levels. There's a lot we can learn from sports psychology.

Jim Loehr, author of *Mentally Tough* and a seasoned researcher in this field, has spent more than 30 years studying athlete behaviour. In one revealing study focusing on tennis players, Loehr made a significant discovery. It wasn't necessarily the most skilled player who emerged victorious in a match. Instead, it was the 16 to 20 seconds between points that held the key. During this brief window, successful tennis professionals engaged in something truly remarkable. They dedicated their time to visualising success. They consciously relaxed and refocused. They took control of their breathing and posture.

The outcome? Their heart rate dropped by a significant 20 beats per minute. They replenished their energy, gaining a competitive edge that consistently translated into winning behaviour on the court. From this observation, Loehr drew a compelling conclusion: a player's 'up time' was only as good as their 'down time'.

As a trader, you have to guard your down time. Make sure you're taking adequate breaks, and watch your sleep, nutrition and exercise habits. To be a finely tuned trading machine, you need to treat yourself like a Ferrari.

Every input you make, every bad habit you break, will take you one step closer to achieving investing success.

Are you an owl or a lark?

It's a common misconception that people make their best decisions in the morning. Research shows this isn't necessarily the case. The best time for decision making is likely to depend on whether you are naturally more alert at a particular time of day—that is, whether you're a morning or an evening person. This is known as your chronotype. When people make a decision at a time that conflicts with their chronotype, they tend to make poorer decisions. And your chronotype is largely decided by your genetics.

What happens when a morning person makes a financial decision in the evening? It seems they're less likely to have considered all of the factors at play. Perhaps they haven't searched for information to help them with that decision, and this will impact their ability to learn from their experience.

When do you make your best decisions? Respect this by reserving important decision making for the time of day when you're most alert.

This is a puzzle where every piece counts. By paying attention to these details, staying disciplined and ensuring every aspect of your investing approach is on point, you create a solid foundation for success in the markets.

Life can often feel like a whirlwind, constantly demanding our attention and energy. It's not uncommon to find ourselves sacrificing rest and relying on energy drinks, coffee and quick snacks to keep us going. Yet we all know it's impossible to maintain a constant state of high energy and alertness. Our bodies and minds need time to recover and recharge.

The demands of trading can be overwhelming. Especially when you're starting out, it may be tempting to dismiss the importance of managing stress levels. Even in the early stages, however, learning to handle pressure and make clear-headed decisions is crucial.

The sleep struggle

Let's talk about insomnia. Around 10 to 15 per cent of us wrestle with chronic sleep problems. So, if you've ever felt like a walking zombie because you haven't had enough sleep, you're definitely not alone. If it's a short-term issue, it can be no more than an inconvenience. When you're in the long-term sleep-deprived club, though, here's what you've signed up for:

- Your productivity and focus take a nosedive.

- Your mood and emotions can be incredibly volatile.

- Your memory and creativity can dip.

- You're more likely to spill coffee on your shirt, crash your car or slip over at work.

- Weight gain, diabetes and heart issues may come knocking at your door.

There are things you can do. Try these top tips for improving your sleep patterns:

- **Create a consistent bedtime routine:** Aim to go to bed and get up at the same time every day, even on weekends. This helps regulate your body's internal clock and the quality of your sleep may improve over time.

- **Limit screen time before bed:** Try to avoid screens for at least an hour before bedtime. The blue light emitted by phones, tablets and computers can interfere with your body's production of melatonin, a hormone that regulates sleep.

- **Create a comfortable sleep environment:** Investing in a good mattress and pillows can make a significant difference to the quality of your sleep. Make sure your bedroom is dark, quiet and at a comfortable temperature.

If these don't work, make an appointment to see a health professional, who can suggest further solutions for you.

It's worth repeating: taking care of yourself, both physically and mentally, directly impacts your performance. By recognising the need for rest, relaxation and self-care, you can better equip yourself to navigate the challenges of being an effective investor with a clear and focused mind.

Pre-think it

Write into your trading plan how you'll handle a knock in the markets. Be careful about catastrophising how big the knock actually is. For example, I can almost guarantee you'll suffer a 15 per cent loss, as it's *really* common.

Consider how you'll react in certain scenarios. Use an 'if...then' statement. This works really well for behaviour modification. For example, 'If I lose 25 per cent of my capital, then I will stop entering new positions, but I will allow the trades I'm in to run until they hit their stop. And I'll contact a higher authority for advice.'

Here are some options about how you could act in this scenario:

If I notice that the 25 per cent drawdown has been triggered, *then* I will:

- stop entering into new positions

- exit any other positions on my stop loss

- continue pyramiding (buying more of a winning position) into current positions that have hit my thresholds

- review my past trades and see whether I didn't follow my rules, and whether there's a particular trade, type of pattern or time frame that is causing a drag on my overall results

- review my findings with a higher authority (such as a trading friend) to see if they can see anything I can't.

Prevention

In his book *Beyond the Investor's Quotient,* Jake Bernstein offers the following prescription for handling stress more effectively:

1. **Stop excessive stress before it starts.** Take regular holidays, and work a reasonable number of hours per day.

2. **Don't try to trade every time frame and every market.** Trade in just a few specific markets and time frames. Try to become an expert in a small number of things.

3. **Don't try to catch every market move**. It is not possible to catch every daily, weekly or monthly move. Specialise in one or two time perspectives.

4. **Keep your goals realistic.** Focus on (1) avoiding losses, (2) increasing equity and (3) making a lot of money. Too many people try to do this in the opposite order.

5. **Don't take the market home with you.** Begin each day fresh.

6. **Find a way to deal with stress and pressure.**

On my podcast Talking Trading, I interviewed Dr Hendrie (Hank) Weisinger, and he gave me the cleverest, most succinct piece of advice. I've cherished it ever since. He told me he has a sign on his desk that reads 'Breathe Slower'. Such a clear instruction, and so easy to implement.

Shift your perception

In life, we encounter moments that test our strength and leave us feeling damaged—whether it's the pain of a broken heart or the disappointment of a financial loss. It's no surprise researchers have discovered that when our heart is broken we can experience physical pain. We describe ourselves as broken, shattered or crushed, and seek solace through sharing our pain with understanding friends.

Society has conditioned us to believe that such 'brokenness' or loss diminishes our value. We perceive it as a flaw that needs to be fixed or hidden away. But what if we dared to see our setbacks in a different light? What if we embraced the notion that they could be catalysts for growth and transformation?

There is a beautiful Japanese art form known as Kintsugi, which means 'golden joinery'. When a precious piece of pottery cracks, instead of discarding it, skilled artists mend it with exquisite precision using lacquer infused with gold or silver. They don't conceal the cracks; they celebrate them. Each piece is painstakingly repaired with a solid filament of gold. The cracks become a cherished part of the artwork, creating a magnificent and incomparable piece that tells a story of resilience and beauty.

Why not apply this wisdom to your own life? Instead of trying to erase the pain of a trade gone wrong or masking the ache you feel, approach your brokenness with reverence. Hold your grief with tenderness, embracing every mistake with patience and, eventually, forgiveness. Most importantly, think of your trading journey with unwavering optimism, honouring the lessons learned along the way and celebrating the growth that emerges from your mistakes. As songwriter and poet Leonard Cohen said, 'There is a crack in everything, that's how the light gets in.'

Use your senses

I vividly recall the pure joy I felt walking out of my corporate job for the last time. Leaving all of the politics, the infighting and the tedium behind, I felt as if by becoming a full-time trader I'd bought back 30 years of my life. I still feel an exhilarating flutter of excitement remembering that feeling.

I also remember the feeling the day I sold my first share that made me more than my finishing salary at my 'real' job. Sublime!

The markets helped me cheat the system (the system that keeps so many shackled to a desk, trying to impress their boss with their latest accomplishment and a 'Look what I did, Mum!' attitude).

Think back to the events in your life that gave you a boost, a shot of energy surging through your system. Recall those feelings to tap into that same burst of energy right now. Surround yourself with sensory reminders — music, food, fragrances. Maybe look at an old photo that shows you performing at the top of your game.

Why? Because when your energy is soaring, you'll get tons of stuff done. Without that energy, you'll head over to the couch and deflate.

When you start to feel yourself dropping into unproductive thought patterns, question your own perceptions. Did you actually have a bad day, or did you have a bad five minutes that you milked for the whole day? If you've been milking life's setbacks, I'll bet you'd benefit from the techniques I've outlined.

You can think your way out of most of your darkest situations. Worth a try, hey?

The pre-mortem method

Whenever I'm presented with a complicated opportunity, I use the pre-mortem method. This is where you imagine the project you're about to be involved with failed abysmally around one year into the future. Think about all of the possible reasons why this could have occurred, as if you were looking back on the entire fiasco. Once you've isolated the potential causes of the catastrophe, review your plan and work out possible ways to plug any holes that could lead to such a crisis in the future. This also works well in a group setting.

Did you have an 'ACE childhood'?

This isn't as good as it sounds. In fact, it defines a childhood marked by trauma and neglect. ACE stands for Adverse Childhood Experiences.

It's possible for the traumas of the past to spill into the present. However, there are scientific ways that can help you reboot your brain and dial down your reactions.

If you were abused or neglected as a child, *it was not your fault.* If you continue living your life through the lens of pain, it will taint everything you do. When you forgive yourself for whatever happened to you in the past, you can work on moving forward.

You don't have to feel great love for the person who abused you, or even speak to them again. But you do need to come to terms with what happened to you. If you don't, those tendrils of neglect and despair will never release you.

You can choose what you feel. The rough, raw, ugly feelings will rise up every so often, but as an adult you can recognise and release them.

Admit that the person you are now was molded by the experiences of your past... and love every part of you. You are no longer insignificant and abandoned. You are a mighty force to be reckoned with, but you have a fearful, unsafe child trapped inside. Comfort that child — it was not their fault. Remind this child that you will protect them now and they can rely on you.

If you need help to recover and accept what has happened to you, seek it out.

And then … release it.

It will improve your investing, but more importantly, it will improve your life.

What can you do that will help you heal? The techniques I'm about to outline have been proven to improve neurogenesis (developing neurons) and synaptogenesis (developing synaptic connections). If you're serious about overcoming your ACE childhood, here are a few things you can try.

Write it down

Write to heal. James Pennebaker from the University of Texas, Austin, gave his students an assignment. He challenged his students to write for at least 20 minutes on four consecutive days about an event they felt was traumatic. He asked them to explore the trauma in intricate detail, recording all of their thoughts and feelings associated with that event. The students wrote down every excruciating detail. 'Really let yourself go,' he told them. 'Explore the event and how it affected you.'

With each subsequent day, as the students explored this method, it became clear that their trauma response was lessening. By the fourth day of writing exclusively about their fears, memories and sometimes terror, the impact of that memory had decreased substantially. Gradually, the students processed their feelings, and the strength of that memory ceased to have as great a hold over them. The stress and negativity they associated with that trauma became more manageable. We'll explore how you can adapt this study from an investing perspective in the next chapter in the section called 'Journal it'.

The results of this study showed the students who underwent this exercise had fewer doctor visits, improved their grades and experienced positive changes in their immune function.

Other methods

Other approaches to helping you recover from trauma include meditation, yoga, CBT (cognitive behavioural therapy), ACT (acceptance commitment therapy), medications prescribed by a professional and support from your community. Some alternative therapies such as EMDR (eye movement desensitisation and reprocessing), EFT Tapping and even some more controversial methods such as the use of psilocybin and psychedelic agents have also been shown to help some people.

If you're looking to rewire your brain using psychedelic agents, it's important to approach this with caution and to be guided appropriately by a trained professional. Be aware that the use and legality of these substances vary by region, so do your homework before jumping in.

Evidence of the success of these methods has been gathered in recent years, but more data is needed. This is an area where you should keep an open mind and seek advice from your health professional.

Embrace the power of recovery and stress prevention, and pre-think how you'll handle some of the blows the market can dish out. Celebrate each small step you make in the right direction, and recognise that even the smallest adjustments can lead to significant improvements, allowing you to grow as a person and as a trader.

Key concepts

- You are responsible for putting together the jigsaw of your personality. You can choose how much you let past experiences affect you. If you're struggling, seek out help so you can rise above the impact of your past.

- Embrace the 'cracks' in your life, because they have the potential to become golden opportunities for growth and transformation. As the Japanese art of Kintsugi celebrates broken pottery by mending it with gold, respect your challenges and setbacks, viewing them as catalysts for success.

Have you suffered a big loss in the markets? Keep reading to hear exactly what to do...

CHAPTER 16

How to handle a big loss

Trading can be a roller-coaster ride. One minute you're raking in profits, and the next you're watching your account dwindle. It will test your patience and make you question your choices. With courage that does not waver and the right mindset, you'll not only weather the reversals but emerge stronger each time.

If you've made a bad move, what can you do so you can continue to trade another day?

It's a huge loss and what makes it worse is you know, deep down, that *you* did this. *Your* actions made this happen.

I've been there.

I know what it's like to struggle for breath as 50-foot waves of regret send you tumbling, fighting, unable to control the outcome. I've felt the shame. The shame that makes you want to stay under the water, even though you know you'll run out of oxygen... because it's quieter under the surface.

But rise you must. Rise and survive.

To begin with, it will seem like another wave strikes you every few minutes. Grief over what you believe signals an erased future. You're driven down to the bottom, then kick off and it's back to the surface. The survival instinct is raw, animal, but you're not at all sure you'll make it.

Over time, though, you notice the waves seem to ease a little. Oh, they're still there, still threatening to drown you as you flounder helplessly, but maybe there's hope, a glint of sun between the waves, a lightening of the sky...

You find your courage, tap into your inner strength and face your fears.

You move forward more confidently now, realising you can still win. You *will* win. And just like that the waves are like ripples in a bathtub. Nothing to fear. Easy to overcome. Yes, your memory of those terrifying waves lives on. But now you're ready for them if they occur again.

Every trader goes through periods when they feel out of sync with the markets and face accumulating losses. You need to study these situations and explore specific techniques to help you get back on track. Begin by analysing the reasons behind your losses, and be open to accepting them as a natural part of the process. Take a closer look at your trading system to determine if any adjustments are needed or if the root cause is your mindset. Are you following a reliable checklist or trading plan? If not, this could be a contributing factor.

Investing can be challenging, frustrating, even exasperating at times. You may find yourself doubting your judgement and questioning your decisions. It takes immense courage to persist, especially during a drawdown period. I am often amazed at how little it takes to stop people dead in their tracks. It doesn't take a mountain to make most people give up on their goals; a pebble will sometimes do. But with determination and the right mindset, you can navigate through these challenges and come out stronger on the other side.

Rather than addressing the possibility your trading system may not be optimal, let's focus on the emotional side. Here are three possible reasons you might be experiencing losses.

Reason 1: Revenge trading

After experiencing a loss, investors often want to get back to where they started and recoup their losses. Acting emotionally, they're less likely to follow careful risk management procedures.

Reason 2: Investing for the thrill

Some traders find themselves captivated by the excitement of investing, even when they're facing losses. They choose, quite irrationally, to continue trading simply for the thrill of it. Trading for excitement poses a real challenge, especially for those who are new to the market.

Research conducted by Gervais and Odean found: 'A trader's expected level of overconfidence increases in the early stages of his career. Then, with more experience, he comes to better recognise his own ability. An overconfident trader trades too aggressively, thereby increasing trading volume and market volatility while lowering his own expected profits.'

With more experience, you can gain a better understanding of your own abilities. As the saying goes, 'There are no old bold traders.' Investing requires emotional maturity and level-headedness.

Reason 3: Fear

Often we let fear hold us back from learning about the markets. What if you stumble and fall? *You might.*

What if you put time into learning about the markets, and discover 'it's not your cup of tea'? *It could happen.*

What if you upset the people around you because you become a raging success? *Also possible.*

You have drive. You have ambition. You have desire. Yet... something is stopping you. Could it be the cold, clammy hand of fear? *Maybe.*

Could it be that you haven't yet found a group of people who believe in you? *Probably.*

Could it be your own image of dazzling success just seems too far away, too obscene, too unlikely? *Most likely.*

But I've got some other questions for you: What if trading does work for you? What difference would this make to your life? What if you give up too early and you never find out what could have been? When does it get to be your time to step up?

In the world of investing, fear can manifest in various forms. There's the fear of incurring losses, the fear of venturing into new territory, the fear of failure, even the fear of others' judgement. But there's another significant fear many investors grapple with: the *fear of success.*

Can you imagine how your life would change if your net worth increased significantly? Being able to visualise your goals is crucial for achieving them. To attain greatness you must first muster the courage to envision it.

Fear has a way of clouding our judgement and leading us to make subjective decisions. Yet if we can recognise and acknowledge the fears we're experiencing, we can minimise their impact.

Extensive research supports the conclusion that training your mind to regulate intense emotions and think with clarity can greatly contribute to your success. By learning to downregulate fear and cultivate an objective mindset, we increase our chances of achieving remarkable results.

It's fine to feel strong emotions, by the way. Actually, it correlates with better trading decisions. The problem arises when you *maintain* those extreme emotions. One study even concluded if you can learn to put your losses in their proper place emotionally and downregulate negative emotions, you're more likely to be profitable.

There are specific actions you can take to think your way out of the struggle with your negative emotions. Then you can shift back into more stable territory so you can experience triumph again.

There's a wise old adage: 'Let me fall if I must fall. The one I become will catch me.'

Post-traumatic stress growth

After a traumatic event, half of all people report at least one positive change (compared with 15 per cent who develop post-traumatic stress disorder).

(continued)

Personal growth after trauma can take five different forms: finding personal strength, gaining appreciation, forming deeper relationships, discovering more meaning in life and seeing new possibilities. Some people say after suffering a trauma, 'The little things don't stress me out now' or 'I'm so grateful for what I *do* have'.

So if you're experiencing trauma — whether personal or in the markets — look for the lesson. It might just change your views about your future. You'll know if this applies to you, but here's a beautiful aphorism from Victor Frankl: 'Suffering ceases to be suffering at the moment it finds meaning.'

What can you do?

Firstly, know you're not alone. Every trader who has been involved in the markets for long enough has experienced losing trades. Here's how to take matters into your own hands.

1. Manage your emotions

Learning how to regulate your emotions has an impact on your risk-taking behaviour. Be aware of the risks so you have a chance of staying in the arena long enough to be successful in the markets. To put it simply, research has confirmed that if you can calm down and regulate your strong emotions, you're more likely to be a sharemarket winner.

2. Tune in to your body's signals

Have you noticed your heart race and your stomach churn when you've made a significant profit or loss? Do you feel your body tense up when you're under pressure or deeply focused? Surprisingly, these physical sensations offer valuable insights for traders.

Being aware of your body can directly impact your profitability.

By cultivating a state of inner stillness and attentiveness to your body's cues, you enhance your ability to refine your actions. Awareness allows you to mentally train yourself, ultimately increasing your chances of success.

In a fascinating study of traders in London, researchers discovered that exceptional traders exhibited a heightened ability to perceive their own heartbeat compared to non-traders. Higher interoceptive awareness correlated with their profitability and could even determine how long they would thrive in the financial markets.

To clarify, *interoception* refers to a sensitivity to the internal state of your body, such as faster heartbeat or hunger pangs, while *introspection* denotes inward reflection on your thoughts and emotions. Both states are indeed crucial for traders.

These research findings suggest that if you cultivate a heightened awareness of your body, you're likely to be more successful as a trader. A sensitivity to how you respond to stress, and indicators such as breathlessness and increased heart rate, can significantly contribute to your success as a trader. This correlation mirrors the strategies employed by athletic coaches to optimise athletes' performance by training their minds through body awareness.

To summarise, developing body awareness and self-awareness of your emotional state, along with the ability to tolerate discomfort during challenging times, will greatly increase your chances of becoming a successful trader. By paying attention to the subtle signals of your body, fine-tuning your responses and honing your mental acuity, you unlock a powerful tool for achieving success as a trader.

3. Reframe it

Skilled investors, consciously or not, employ reappraisal psychology, which involves mentally reframing an event to diminish the negative emotions associated with it. This practice is a crucial aspect of emotional regulation.

For instance, you can reframe your losses as a necessary part of the journey. Recognise that every trader encounters losses. You're not nervous… you're excited. You're not worried… you're concentrating on achieving the best outcome.

If you attempt to suppress your emotional response to a loss or gain, this won't help you in the long run. Training yourself in the art of reappraisal can significantly enhance your overall performance as an investor. It can help you develop stronger decision-making skills and cultivate resilience in the face of challenges.

4. Use introspection

Another crucial aspect is introspection—taking the time to reflect deeply, without distractions, on your losses and profits. It may be uncomfortable, but the effort is worthwhile. Creating a quiet environment and maintaining focused attention are essential for this introspective work.

By immersing yourself in this process and honestly examining areas for improvement without succumbing to distractions or evading uncomfortable emotions, you increase your chances of becoming a high-performance trader. Introspection helps you to uncover valuable insights and make meaningful adjustments to your trading strategies and mindset, ultimately enhancing your overall abilities.

It's a fine line, though. Thinking but not acting, or acting without thinking—both are recipes for disaster. Think hard and critically, then make a plan to re-engage with the markets.

5. Journal it

Develop the habit of writing down your thoughts on paper in what some psychologists call a morning journal.

Psychoanalyst Carl Jung saw journaling as a way to access your unconscious mind by writing down your unedited thoughts first thing in the morning in a free-form, stream of consciousness manner without any intervention by your conscious mind.

Many successful people keep journals. Perhaps most famously, Leonardo da Vinci filled tens of thousands of pages with sketches and musings on his art, inventions, observations and ideas. Albert Einstein amassed more than 80 000 pages of notes in his lifetime. John Adams, the second president of the United States, filled 51 journals during his lifetime.

And you can use your journal to help you recover from a big loss in the markets. Let's break it down, day by day:

Day 1: Let yourself fully express your pain. Write about it in excruciating detail, allowing your emotions to flow onto the pages. Don't hold back. Embrace those strong feelings.

Day 2: Shift your focus and reflect on what you did well in the situation. Also, consider what you would do differently if given the chance in the future. This exercise helps you find insights and lessons to carry forward.

Day 3: Take another dive into your emotions. Describe any lingering pain you haven't addressed yet, without rehashing the same details. This is an opportunity to release any additional emotions related to the event. Force yourself to write about new pain points.

Day 4: Challenge yourself to explore the perspective that the situation might have been entirely your fault. What valuable lessons do you want to learn from it? If it was totally your fault, then sit with it. Document your stuff-ups and say what, specifically, you'd do differently if you had your time over again. This exercise encourages growth and personal accountability.

Day 5: Shift your focus to self-care. Explore ways to soothe your body and mind during this healing process. Consider activities or practices that will bring you comfort and restore your wellbeing.

Day 6: Take a journey into the future. Imagine it's five years from now, and reflect on how that painful experience served as a turning point in your life. Paint a vivid picture of the positive changes and growth you have achieved. This technique, known as *future pacing*, can be incredibly powerful.

Day 7: Review the previous six days of journaling. Allow yourself to feel the grief and acknowledge its presence. Don't shy away from it. Then consider how this process of reflection and introspection can guide you towards a brighter future.

By engaging with your emotions and experiences in this way, you create an opportunity for deep healing and personal growth.

Even if you haven't started investing in the markets yet, it's essential you start to work on your mind. When traders begin, they often think success will come easily to them. They underestimate the importance of the task at hand. Don't make this mistake. Be prepared for all eventualities by educating yourself, developing your mind and developing success habits.

'Courage doesn't always roar,' observes Mary Anne Radmacher. 'Sometimes courage is the little voice at the end of the day that says I'll try again tomorrow.'

Key concepts

- Embrace the waves. Trading tests your patience and your choices, but with the right mindset you can weather the storm and emerge stronger.

- Analyse the reasons why your loss occurred, and make adjustments to guide your future actions.

- Manage your emotions—tune into your body's signals, reframe your loss and use introspection.

Many savvy investors swear that using affirmations can make all the difference to their results. Here's how to do this so you can maximise your chances of success.

CHAPTER 17

As close as you'll get to a quick fix

Welcome to the roller-coaster ride of being a trader! It's a world filled with thrilling ups and terrifying downs. Just when you think you have it all figured out, BAM! A new twist throws your plans out the window. It's like navigating a maze where the walls keep shifting. Here's how to excel with flair using the power of affirmations.

When you're a trader, everything can seem like a threat. One moment you're celebrating a profitable trade, feeling like a champion; the next, defying logic and reason, everything takes a nosedive. It's enough to make your head spin!

It's a constant battle against the unknown, with threats lurking around every corner. But hey, that's what makes investing both exhilarating and challenging. The market loves to keep you on your toes, testing your resilience and adaptability.

Even the most ironclad rules sometimes fall short, leaving you scratching your head and wondering, 'What now?' It's those unexpected curveballs that separate the best from the rest.

They know how to roll with the punches and find new strategies when the old ones don't cut it.

When this happens, the savviest traders have a secret weapon. It's called 'getting some damned help'!

I love this passage from Haruki Murakami's novel *Kafka on the Shore*:

> 'And once the storm is over, you won't remember how you made it through, how you managed to survive. You won't even be sure whether the storm is really over. But one thing is certain. When you come out of the storm, you won't be the same person who walked in. That's what this storm's all about.'

If you're in the storm, waiting for your world to come crashing down, know that a multitude of other successful traders have been there before you and have moved beyond it. They've been through those tumultuous winds and survived to trade another day.

So how do you start to downregulate your emotions when everything seems so threatening? First…

What are you saying to yourself?

Let's talk about the power of your inner dialogue and how it can shape your perception of threat in the wild world of markets. Brace yourself, because it's about to get intriguing.

In a wild study in 2011, Harber and associates dug deep into this topic. (The research involved live tarantulas and victims… oops, I mean 'study subjects'.) The researchers discovered something unexpected and fascinating. It seems the participants' self-worth played a major role in how close and menacing the spider appeared to them, and 'the more self-worth participants experienced, the less close the tarantula appeared to them'.

For investors, this means if you can boost your self-worth, you're more likely to evaluate threats calmly and without hysteria. The goal with investing is to objectively assess threats, rather than jump at your own shadow. So it stands to reason, anything you can do to help yourself with this should improve your results.

And here's the good news. You have the ability to boost your self-worth using affirmations. Let's check your technique so you're doing this optimally.

Affirmations

Affirmations are positive statements or phrases repeated regularly in order to influence your beliefs and attitudes, and promote self-confidence and a positive mindset. They are a mighty weapon in your arsenal. Those uplifting statements also help you detach yourself from perceived threats. They can really help your trading. By practising self-affirmations, you can develop a healthy dose of objectivity. This may sound strange, but it's backed by research, so it's worth a shot, hey?

Affirmations can help to block out those nagging voices that sometimes tell us we're destined for failure, and replace them with positive thoughts.

For the ideal affirmation, follow these steps:

- **Set a specific goal.** Make sure you keep them in present tense, and take out any qualifications (kinda, sorta, more or less) that lessen the impact of your statement. The subconscious mind doesn't understand the future. It only 'gets' now. The more you can make it as if it's happening now, the better.

- **Write it down, and repeat daily.** You could start with this basic format:

  'I, [insert your name], have achieved/done/accomplished [insert your goal].'

- **Make it powerful and vibrant.** Add emotion, intensity and vivid imagery to make it pop, as if you're already living that reality.

- **Stay realistic.** If your goal has a specific time frame, ensure it's realistic and achievable. Winning the next Olympic freestyle event might be a stretch if you can barely dog paddle. Keep your desires grounded in reality.

- **Be positive and concrete.** Avoid using words like 'want' or 'try'. Express your affirmations in a positive and concrete way. Make it crystal clear you're already on the path to success.

- **Carry them with you.** Write your affirmations on flashcards and make them your trusty companions. Pin them up on your mirror and carry them with you to read during idle moments. Fold them into your daily routine, like reading them while brushing your teeth. Use them as your screen saver. To keep things fresh, try using different coloured cards and updating your affirmations periodically.

- **Stretch and believe.** Push yourself with affirmations, but be sure you believe it's possible to achieve those outcomes. If you struggle to believe them after a few days, adjust the wording. Visualise your affirmations and immerse yourself in the experience by engaging your senses — touch, taste, sight, sound and smell. Make it real in your mind.

Do this ... not that

A weak affirmation:

'I must believe in myself and my judgement if I expect to make a living from investing.'

More powerful:

'I make an exceptional living from investing, and I believe in myself.'

or

'I am thriving in my trading career because my judgement is excellent and I believe in myself.'

or

'I consciously choose to trade for a living, and my self-belief is rock solid.'

See the difference? By crafting affirmations like these, you shape and elevate your self-belief. They serve as catalysts for achieving the goals you desire. By focusing on the positive and concrete aspects, you reinforce your commitment and set yourself up for success.

The fine print

While affirmations can work wonders, consistency is key. Research suggests they are most effective when used proactively, *before* you find yourself knee-deep in trouble. Think of them as a shield of resilience, protecting you from potential chaos. As part of your psychological fitness journey, it's important to plan and stay ahead of the game.

Affirmations don't bring results overnight. They require dedication and sustained effort for the long haul.

This is your opportunity to create a powerful internal dialogue that propels you toward success. Embrace the journey, stay consistent and let those affirmations work their magic. You've got this.

Key concepts

- If you can boost your self-worth, you're more likely to evaluate threats objectively. Using affirmations can help you achieve this goal.

- When writing affirmations, use the present tense and make sure they're specific, realistic and positive. Repetition, and using affirmations before a crisis occurs, count.

There's more to achieving great results than just using affirmations. Is willpower a factor? Let's look at this topic next.

CHAPTER 18

Debunking the myth of willpower

Is relying on willpower the best way to make enduring life changes? Here we'll look at a fresh perspective on how you can harness your inner drive.

Imagine striving for a promotion, mastering trading skills, shedding those extra kilos or conquering a half marathon. Can sheer inspiration and willpower alone guarantee success?

Studies reveal that we possess a finite reserve of willpower that is susceptible to depletion, like an overworked muscle. As we progress through the day, our willpower dwindles due to its gradual expenditure, highlighting the phenomenon known as ego depletion. This notion, put forward by researchers Haan and Veldhuizen, emphasises that self-control and other cognitive processes rely on a limited mental resource pool that can be exhausted.

There are compelling reasons to cultivate and enhance your willpower. A study conducted by Hoffer and Gildings found that individuals with greater willpower tend to achieve higher education levels, earn higher incomes, secure better employment opportunities, experience lower rates of criminality and poverty, and are less likely to be obese. Interestingly, research suggests training willpower in one area of life can extend its capacity to other domains. For instance, athletes who performed a willpower-draining task exhibited less depletion and greater persistence in solving an unsolvable puzzle compared to non-athletes.

However, what if you're not an athlete or an exceptional performer in other aspects of your life unrelated to investing? Does this imply an inevitable failure in the financial markets? Are you destined to never attain high performance as a trader?

The good news

Author and cartoonist, Scott Adams, found that relying heavily on willpower is not a sustainable practice. He suggests that avoiding situations where you are faced with the choice between pleasure and deprivation is key to conserving your willpower, as pleasure tends to prevail in such circumstances. Focus on the process, not the outcome.

This highlights the significance of effectively managing your environment to increase your chances of excelling in the markets. Additionally, even in the context of addiction recovery, strategies play a more crucial role than sheer willpower. Research indicates that individuals with addiction don't lack willpower, but they benefit from developing strategies and processes to preserve willpower through controlling their environment.

Leverage this research to enhance your skills

Here are four techniques you can use to keep you running towards your goals:

1. Harness samvega

My neighbour Roma was 92 when she passed away. I was with her at the end. Her final gift to me was the last smile that ever graced her face.

An orphan, she worked as a domestic helper for six and a half days a week from when she was 13 until she was 28 years old. I was mesmerised by her stories and how she packed her life full of adventures, despite her difficult upbringing.

She took up mountain climbing in her fifties and ballroom dancing in her eighties, for which she received a bronze medal (apparently a big deal in ballroom dancing circles) in her nineties. She had lovingly hand-sewn on every sequin on her ball gown. Every feather that flowed gracefully as she moved across the dance floor was a tribute to her character.

In our last conversation she told me my gravestone will show two dates with a dash in between. 'Everyone's "dash" is really their life,' she said. 'Make sure you pack yours with experiences that are precious to you.'

What does your 'dash' look like so far?

Have you achieved what you were hoping to… or are you still *waiting* for adventures to happen?

Trading practice is characterised by a slow, sometimes imperceptible gathering of skills. Because progress can seem slow, it's not unusual to lack motivation. So when that happens, how do we re-energise?

The Pali word *samvega* refers to the stark realisation that death can happen at any moment. You never know when the sand is going to run out of the hourglass. This thought isn't supposed to scare us. It's meant to wake us up to life's preciousness, so we can revel in all it brings, and we can commit to the priorities in our life.

We have a tendency not to think about our impermanence, as the idea of death can make us uncomfortable. But we are here for a blink. A flash.

We may think that a good life is one in which we are the sum total of our accomplishments. From a mindfulness perspective, a good life is one that is experienced fully, with an open heart.

In the words of Steven Pinker, 'Nothing gives life more purpose than the realisation that every moment of consciousness is a precious and fragile gift.'

Sometimes I wonder what would have happened if I hadn't learned how to trade. What future would have been blocked off?

I know one thing: if I was working corporate hours now, I wouldn't be able to be as involved in my kids' lives. That precious half hour when they come home and vie for my attention, 'motor-mouthing' about all the things they've done during the day. That alone makes all the sacrifices around learning about the markets worth it.

*Fast-forward into **your** future. If you don't choose trading now, what choices will that decision block off for you?*

I don't know your reason for wanting to trade. Perhaps you're looking to flee your current position, or maybe you're running towards the bounty trading holds for those who master it. I do know that unless you can define your motivation — be it carrot or stick — your chances of succeeding as a trader will be limited. What's your motivation? Write it down in your notebook to guide your future actions.

You'll either run towards your goals or escape from something that fills you with dread. That's what it takes to be an effective trader.

2. Be careful about unrealistic fantasies

Gabrielle Oettingen, Professor of Psychology at NYU, explains, 'The more positively people fantasise about their desired futures, the *less* effort they invest and the *less* successful they are in realising these futures. However, when fantasies about a desired future are complemented with a clear sense of reality, people find the direction and energy needed to realise their fantasies.'

The graduates who daydreamed about future success ended up sending out fewer job applications, getting fewer job offers and earning a lower salary.

People kicking off a weight-loss journey, dreaming of a supermodel bod, often found themselves not shedding as many kilos as they'd hoped, and were more likely to put the weight back on again.

Outstanding investing comes from within, tempered by an effective dose of realistic thinking. It involves pre-planning how you'll react to obstacles that stand between you and your ultimate success.

Mental contrasting

One technique to help you achieve exceptional results is called *mental contrasting*.

Gabrielle Oettingen developed a scientifically proven tool called WOOP (for **W**ish **O**utcome **O**bstacle **P**lan). Using this tool, you pre-visualise the things that could stop you from reaching your goal, then create an advance plan to overcome these obstacles.

Here an 'if... then' plan can be really useful. If this happens, then you'll take this action. For example, if you experience five losses in the markets in a row, then you'll check in with your mentor to see if there's a problem.

This isn't negative thinking. It's factoring the obstacles you're likely to face into your visualisation, and planning around them.

Traders must be ready for every twist. They plan for the worst. They set stops. They are pragmatic. Exceptional traders know their worst-case scenario and know when they need to step aside from the markets. It's about planning for contingencies and embracing risk management.

---

3. Create a success environment

Dr Libby Sander, future of work expert at Bond University, states, 'The effect of our spaces on our physical and psychological states is more profound than we realise.' She explains, 'Where we work must enable experiences that match the state required for the work ... Instead of focusing on the workplace, our focus should be on the work state we are trying to achieve.'

Creating the right environment for success is incredibly important but often overlooked. Your surroundings can make a big difference to how well you perform as a trader. Think about where you work best and can stay focused for longer periods. Arrange your trading desk to support your performance and minimise distractions.

Jeff Haden, author of *The Motivation Myth*, suggests tweaking your environment to avoid impulsive actions. For example, if pesky phone notifications distract you, turn them off. If your pet bird's squawking messes with your thinking, relocate it to another room while you trade.

Anything that helps you stay focused will boost your chances of success.

A focused fool can achieve more than a distracted genius.

4. Follow a checklist

Many believe they can rely on their memory when following their trading plan and don't see the need for a written checklist. Research, however, suggests checklists can significantly enhance performance of complex tasks. In the medical field, for example, there is evidence of the positive impact of checklists on patient outcomes, with studies showing reduced morbidity and mortality rates following surgery. One revealing research study concluded, 'Safety checklists have been shown to impact positively on patient morbidity and mortality following surgery.'

All of this takes time and effort. However, if you can stay in the arena longer and mitigate the damaging effects of stress, you're more likely to be successful in the markets.

Rely on systems and not willpower. Develop strategies and routines to help you become disciplined and focused.

To sum up, never forget that you're a complex creature who nonetheless has very simple needs:

- **Eat on purpose.** You need good fuel to really excel, so avoid that greasy cheeseburger and grab a salad.

- **Exercise on purpose.** Without treating your body well, you'll lack the energy to continue pursuing your goals. See to your issues of wear and tear, and listen to your body. You might be surprised by what it has to tell you.

- **Relax on purpose.** Give yourself time just to ponder the world, away from the hustle and bustle, so you can live with gusto.

- **Sleep on purpose.** Without great sleep, you'll become psychotic. (I'm not making that up!) Get to bed at a reasonable hour so you're not wrecked the next day.

- **Play on purpose.** Don't just plonk down on the couch and watch TV. Pursue activities that get your blood pumping, that give you a little shivery thrill of excitement just thinking about them. Dump just one of your favourite TV shows a night — buy back an hour, and do something incredible with it.

- **Pursue your ambitions on purpose.** Run after them, arms flailing, hair flying, ready to knock down any wall in your way. You owe it to yourself.

Do this for one day and you'll feel great.

Do it for one week and you'll have a spring in your step and rediscover your enthusiasm.

Do it for a lifetime and you'll really have lived a purposeful life.

Key concepts

- You can exhaust your self-control, which is why you need more than willpower if you're going to achieve your goals.

- The power of your purpose can push you forward even when your willpower has dried up.

- Pre-plan how you'll cope with life's obstacles. Create a plan in advance to overcome life's speed bumps.

- Think about where you work best and can stay focused for longer periods. Your success environment can help you avoid distractions and hit your goals.

Key 5 will reveal why inspiration is essential for keeping your investing powering forward...

KEY 5

Motivation

Use inspiration to drive your results forward

Inspiration—that magical force that drives you into action—holds the key to unlocking your potential. It's the spark of brilliant insight, the 'aha' moment, when you see new possibilities and feel a surge of enthusiasm in your bones.

Without inspiration, trading and investing can feel merely repetitive. So just what is inspiration, and how can it help you become a better trader?

Researchers have uncovered three powerful characteristics of inspiration. Firstly, *evocation* stirs up emotions, which is essential to experiencing inspiration. Secondly, *transcendence* elevates you beyond your mental limitations. Thirdly, *approach motivation* means you strive for something positive (rather than avoiding something negative). It's like a lightning bolt from outside yourself, lifting you beyond the ordinary and flooding you with vivid and concrete awareness. It lights a fire under your trading aspirations.

But here's the key. It's essential to seek inspiration from diverse sources. Explore new avenues, find inspiration in unexpected places and fuel your journey with an ever-flowing wellspring of energy.

Also, remember to check your attitude or you won't experience the benefits of inspiration. Think for a moment:

- Do you feel a surge of inspiration when you hear about another trader's success in the markets? Or do you find yourself dismissing it, thinking it's only possible for 'born traders'?

- When you come across stories of market wizards living the high life, does a voice in your head say, 'Well, that's not for me. I'm happy with far less. Anyway, they must have some special talent.'

- And what about those who have made the leap to trade full-time in less time than you? Do you feel a twinge of jealousy? Do you silently curse them?

These reactions reveal something crucial about your mindset. They indicate whether you're operating from a fixed mindset or a growth mindset. If you find yourself feeling threatened by the success of others, it's a clear sign your mindset needs to shift. As soon as you become aware of this you can make the jump to being inspired.

Upward comparison

We constantly compare ourselves to others. It's part of being human. We compare ourselves to people we consider superior to us in some way. This upward form of comparison can inspire us or degrade us. How we react is a choice. We can choose to consider people further down the path positively or negatively.

We also compare ourselves to people we consider beneath us. This can cause us to feel superior and provide an ego boost — and possibly remind us of how far we've come. It can also act as a cautionary tale: we take steps so we don't behave like those we're comparing ourselves to.

You can't escape comparing yourself to others, but you can change your perception about how this is done so you benefit.

Keep reading to be inspired by the psychology of athletes and investors...

CHAPTER 19

Game on — exploring the winning mindsets of athletes and investors

Step into the captivating worlds of high-performance sports and investing. There are surprising parallels between athletes and investors, and now you can discover the secrets to success in both realms. Get inspired and equipped with valuable strategies to elevate your game. This is your ticket to unlocking your inner champion in both arenas.

To learn a new skill effectively, it is important to find someone to emulate and to constantly top up your levels of inspiration. Tony Robbins says, 'If you want to be a success, find someone who has achieved what you want and copy them.'

Inspirational mentors don't have to come only from the trading arena.

Let me share a story with you, one that involves a legendary swimmer you're likely familiar with — Michael Phelps. But here's something you might not know. Behind his astonishing 23 world records, a mindset method played a crucial role. The lessons for investors are undeniable.

Enter Bob Bowman, the brilliant coach who recognised Michael's extraordinary potential back when Phelps was in grade 5. He knew physical training alone could only take Michael so far. That's when Bob imparted a powerful mantra to his young protégé — 'It takes what it takes.'

Bob understood the importance of mental preparation and the impact it could have on performance. He encouraged Michael to envision himself swimming in the Olympics, to set goals for the year ahead and even for his next training session. He introduced Michael to what he called 'The Movie'.

The Movie

More than just an idea, it was a complete mental visualisation of winning the race, playing out in Michael's mind in vivid detail. And here's the fascinating part: science tells us that mental practice such as 'The Movie' activates mirror neurons in your brain, engaging the same circuits as if you were actually experiencing the activity in real life. These neurons help us understand and empathise with others, like feeling joy when watching a friend succeed or flinching when they face a mishap.

In other words, by mentally rehearsing success, Michael was not only preparing his mind but also triggering his brain to wire itself for peak performance. This secret weapon fuelled his extraordinary achievements.

During the 2008 Beijing Olympics, both Bob and Michael were hoping for a ground-breaking world record. They had their movies all lined up. What they hadn't planned for was an unforeseen obstacle that would put their preparation to the ultimate test.

As the race began, disaster struck for Michael.
His goggles started to fill up with water,
impairing his vision.

By the halfway point, he found himself swimming blindly with stinging eyes, and uncertainty clouding his mind.

But here's where the power of Michael's mind truly shone through. During countless practice sessions in the pool, he had grown tired of his mental movies always being perfect. Seeking to push his boundaries, he had deliberately imagined disasters of every kind. And he had rehearsed these very scenarios in his mind, over and over, in his mental 'disaster movies'.

Michael could barely see because his goggles were full of water. Without clear vision, he had to find a way around the obstacles that threatened to hinder his performance.

Michael knew it took exactly 20 strokes to reach the wall. And what happened next was nothing short of extraordinary. Against all odds, Michael not only won the race but also achieved a world record and earned the gold medal. His swim was perfect precisely because he had pre-rehearsed the challenges and devised strategies to overcome them.

Michael's story teaches us a valuable lesson.

By envisioning and preparing for the worst-case
scenarios, you can cultivate a mindset of resilience
and adaptability. It's about being ready for whatever
comes your way, including unexpected obstacles.

Positive thinking can foul you up

Your mindset and the way you approach your goals will significantly impact your outcomes. However, you might be surprised to learn that excessive positive thinking, associated with unwavering optimism, may not always be the best method.

As we learned in the previous chapter, university graduates who indulged in overly positive fantasies about their future success ended up sending out fewer job applications, receiving fewer job offers and earning less income two years later. Similarly, individuals embarking on weight-loss journeys who envisioned themselves with a perfect physique, often faced challenges and tended to regain lost weight or struggle to lose as much weight as initially anticipated. And those who dreamt of the perfect relationship often found themselves feeling more isolated.

When you mentally simulate your desired outcomes in an excessively positive manner, you can trick your mind into believing you have already achieved success. As a result, you may not devote as much effort or energy towards the goal itself.

This doesn't mean you should abandon all positive thinking. It can be beneficial in many ways, providing motivation, resilience and a positive outlook. But it's essential to strike a balance and avoid excessive fantasising that may hinder your progress.

It can be more effective to combine realistic optimism with a mindset that acknowledges potential challenges and setbacks along the way.

Feel it

Let's face it, most of us suck at expressing our feelings. You've been taught since you were a kid to bury them down deep. But here's a more effective strategy. When you're hurt, let those feelings burst out, and overflow if necessary. Just sit with them and hold yourself in grief. If you ignore how you're feeling, those feelings will lurk in the shadows and take control of your life.

Martin Luther King Jr. said, 'Take your burden, take your grief and look at it, don't run from it.' Wise words. Take a good hard look at yourself and ask, 'How can I turn this liability into something valuable?'

Picture this: You made a loss because you didn't obey your stop loss. Or you messed up big time and bought the wrong number of shares. Allow the shame to wash over you. Because if you push down those feelings and ignore the lessons, you're bound to repeat the same mistakes, only next time they'll be even bigger and more damaging.

When you're going through hell, keep on going. It's not the time to curl up and suck your thumb. Observe, keep moving and making decisions — even if they're not perfect, it's better than making no decision at all. So embrace those feelings, learn from them and keep pushing forward. Visualise how you'll respond if things go wrong and you'll be better equipped to handle it. You'll be ready to respond more quickly and decisively when bad things happen.

The roads are littered with roadkill, their indecisiveness sealing their fate. They hesitated and paid the ultimate price. They didn't think ahead.

If you want to make serious profits, you can't treat being an investor like a hobby. No, no, no. You have to take it as seriously as an athlete preparing for the Olympics. If investing is at the bottom of your priority list, let me tell you straight up, you'll never earn a substantial income from the markets. It's as simple as that.

Draw motivation and method from other psychological fields in your pursuit of high performance in the markets. Judiciously borrowing the techniques used by others is a great way to feed your own trading inspiration.

Key concepts

- Emulate successful mentors: To learn a new skill effectively, find someone to copy and stay inspired. Seek mentors not only in but also outside your field, as valuable insights can come from unexpected sources.

- Balance positive thinking: While positive thinking can provide motivation and resilience, excessive fantasising about success may hinder progress. Acknowledge potential obstacles and challenges while visualising desired outcomes.

- Feel it to heal it: Don't bury your feelings; rather, embrace them to learn valuable lessons. Allowing yourself to process emotions after a loss or setback can contribute to a mindset of resilience and adaptability. By acknowledging and learning from your feelings, you can grow and make better decisions in the future.

- Take investing seriously: Treat trading as a serious business and prioritise it. Invest time, effort and dedication to achieve businesslike success.

Paper trading is where you don't place money into the markets but you record every position you'd like to enter and exit on paper. So is this a good way to learn about the specifics of the markets? Or should we dive right in, and learn with our own money on the line? Let's find out in the next chapter...

CHAPTER 20

Feel the pain and do it anyway

Will paper trading help you in the long run, or is it better just to dive into your first trade? We'll explore this question in this chapter...

It seems like we spend our whole life trying to avoid pain. We learn from an early age that the oven shouldn't be touched. How do we know that? Usually because we reached out our podgy little toddler hands while Mum wasn't watching, and received a burn for our efforts. Pain makes us withdraw, cry and sometimes get angry. It makes us less likely to repeat the action that caused the pain. The lesson taught by pain is embedded with remarkable speed, way ahead of Mum's verbal warnings. Pain serves a purpose.

How you react to physical violence can give you an insight into your true self. Your external façade is stripped away and you find out whether you are more likely to cower in the corner, seek avoidance or summon the strength to hit back. Martial artists know that to train to an elite level, they must be willing to experience pain.

If the pain, or even the thought of pain, interferes with your ability to function, then you have a problem.

The slap test

When Robert Redenbach and Graham Kuerschner trained police and military personnel in the lead-up to the Sydney Olympics, they used a controversial but highly effective tool. The course organisers believed that it is only by being subjected to pain that people can combat their fear and maintain their focus, whatever the challenge.

During the five-day course, participants were subjected to the 'slap test', during which they would kneel on the ground without a shirt and their partner would slap them on the chest and back repeatedly with an open palm, as many times as possible in five seconds. (Wow... what a fun course, hey?)

Reactions to the slaps varied. Some guys with vast amounts of bravado crumbled. Others who didn't look like they would be up to the task coped admirably. Given that they were all members of the elite police or military forces, it is interesting that it was almost impossible to judge who would be able to cope with this type of pain test. There are lessons for us as traders in using pain to our advantage.

Paper trading

Rather than risking 'real' money in the markets, many traders begin by paper trading. They write down every detail of their trade in a trading diary, including their position sizing, stop loss, and profit-taking procedures. They imagine they're really going to take the trade, record their entry price and monitor the stock over time. This has the effect of letting the trader gain some valuable, risk-free experience using their investing signals and processes.

There are a couple of problems with this practice. The main one is that there is no pain involved when an incorrect decision is made. The lessons to be learned through paper trading are never adequately reinforced. The pain of losing money and the pleasure of making a profitable trade are not experienced by the paper trader. There's nothing like the pain you feel after having money mercilessly ripped out of your account to help your learning curve!

Paper trading sometimes allows people to kid themselves that they are actually more skilled than reality would suggest. They tend to remember the 'good' trades and forget the ones that are less than favourable. By trying to avoid pain, they are actually prolonging their own learning cycle.

Be aware, when investing with real money, some traders need to go through a catastrophe to finally get their own attention and make an effort to improve their system. Psychologists call this 'one-trial learning'. That bad trade is so devastating that it results in an instant change in behaviour — painful but effective. A quick whack to the side of the head can sometimes be the best thing to happen to you, as long as your head doesn't get completely knocked off in the process. So make sure you go about your entry into the market sensibly by formulating your trading plan before getting started.

It's wise to try at least a few trades on paper at first, however, especially if you're just starting out. This will give you a chance to learn how these instruments work before risking your capital. Just remember to limit the number of trades you intend to make and the time you will need to make those trades. Set yourself a deadline for putting real money into the market. Work on your trading plan as ferociously as if you were planning to take over a multimillion-dollar company.

No matter how clever we are at paper trading, there's nothing like putting your own money into the market and experiencing the ultimate emotional roller-coaster. Our emotions have a very real impact on our ability as traders. Allow yourself to feel the pain of defeat, as you will make losses initially, especially as you begin investing using a new system (because your initial stops will be hit quicker than your trailing stops).

Alongside pain comes pleasure, profits and the knowledge that you are improving your skills. Iron out the visible flaws in your plan before jumping in, but don't be afraid of a little pain. It's truly the quickest way to learn and to become an effective trader.

Key concepts

- Pain can sometimes be our most effective teacher. If you shelter yourself from the pain, sometimes you won't learn essential lessons.
- Putting your own money in the markets can be the quickest way to grasp what it takes to be successful.

One of the key aspects of inspiration is *approach motivation.* In the next chapter we're going to dive into this vital area...

CHAPTER 21

Approach your goal setting the right way

Framing goals as *approach goals* (striving for something positive) or *avoidance goals* (avoiding something negative) can impact our motivation and feelings when we achieve those goals. Let's delve into the intriguing connection between goal framing, achievement and emotions.

In the summer of 2012 Allyson Felix stood poised at the Olympic 200-meter-sprint starting blocks, fuelled by a burning desire for a gold medal. The weight of her previous silver medals hung heavy on her mind, driving her to declare, 'I can't lose again.'

And in less than 22 seconds she claimed the coveted gold medal.

But as the thrill of victory washed over her, an unexpected emotion crept in — instead of the elation you'd expect on winning a gold medal, what she felt was relief. She realised she had been fuelled more by the desire to 'not lose' than by the goal to 'win'.

Approach goals vs avoidance goals

The way you frame your goals can determine how you feel *after* you have achieved them. Motivation researchers study approach goals and avoidance goals. Winning the 200-metre race is an approach goal. 'Not losing' is an avoidance goal.

Research reveals an intriguing aspect of goal-setting: if we focus solely on avoidance goals, we don't feel especially fulfilled when we achieve them. This is a problem, because for habit formation to truly cement, a perceived reward is essential.

When your focus centres primarily on avoiding certain outcomes, the emotional boost you typically experience — known as *positive affect* — upon accomplishing a goal is dampened. Instead of deriving satisfaction and fulfilment, we may feel drained.

Allyson Felix's experience is a prime example. Having fixated on avoiding a specific outcome in the 200-metres race, winning the gold failed to bring her the genuine sense of satisfaction she had anticipated.

It all came down to what drove her and how she framed her goal.

In some ways, the results might be the same, independent of whether you set an approach goal or an avoidance goal. However, when you lean into an approach goal, the rewards you experience will feel richer. Yes, you need to plan for the worst. But you also need to visualise how you'll feel when you succeed.

Mark Spitz first gained fame in swimming at the 1968 Olympics in Mexico City, coming home with two gold, one silver and one bronze medal. Despite this outstanding result, Mark was disgusted with his performance. He knew he could do better.

In a series of press interviews, he told the world he would come home from the 1972 Munich Olympics with seven gold medals. Mark set his standards high, emotionally visualised his future and imagined how he'd feel when he won. He committed to his training program with confidence. He stretched, but also maintained a healthy grip on reality.

Mark achieved his goal in 1972, setting several world records in the process. Behind this apparent overnight success was an amazing dedication to training. Mark's visualisations gave him the strength to carry on, year after year, lifting weights, training and swimming in preparation for his goal. It goaded him into action.

Effective visualisations

To bring your visualisations to fruition, you need to focus on them at least once a day, every day. Visualise your goal in the present tense, as if it is happening right now. Make it as detailed as possible, imagine the emotions you will feel and picture exactly how you will perform.

As when writing effective affirmations, the mind cannot imagine a negative. For example, aiming to visualise not getting stressed is far less powerful than imagining you are calm and serene while taking a trade. Whatever visualisations you choose, make them positive so your mind can grasp exactly the type of behaviour you want to recreate in the future.

So do you sprint towards financial independence or jog away from the spectre of financial need? It turns out there's another concept that's probably a better guide for goal-setting traders.

Mastery goals

A mastery goal is widely regarded as the pinnacle of an approach goal. Dweck and Leggett explain that mastery goals reflect an individual's determination to maximise learning. You strive to understand and apply your knowledge.

Take students studying for an exam. By embracing the mindset of mastering the material, rather than merely avoiding failure or getting a good mark, they can grasp and retain a greater amount of information. When motivation stems from the desire to achieve mastery rather than seeking external validation (such as the appreciation of their teachers or extrinsic rewards), students are more likely to succeed in their aims.

In the markets, extrinsic rewards could include achieving a particular percentage return or a certain level of profit. Intrinsic rewards may include the warm, positive feelings of accomplishment you experience when you make your first trade, follow your trading plan to the letter or complete that online course you started so long ago.

What sort of goals should you set?

The accomplishment of a mastery goal involves a high degree of intrinsic motivation. Intrinsic motivation is commonly defined as 'doing something for its own sake' — for example, when you learn about investing just because you want to. There isn't a driving force of financial need making you want to be a trader. You're just fascinated by the financial markets and you want to learn as much as you can about them.

In trading, intrinsic motivation arises from a genuine fascination with the markets and a desire to immerse yourself in learning.

There is no external pressure to please others or to meet their expectations. It's a personal journey driven by your own goals and aspirations.

Intrinsic motivation

Intrinsic motivation pushes you to become an expert on the key principles of investing. These include implementing checklists and writing a trading plan that clearly outlines entry and exit strategies, as well as position sizing. You'll also strive to master your trading platform, charting tools and the specific trading discipline you choose, be it technical analysis or fundamental analysis. (For more on how to use technical analysis skills using formulas and indicators, as well as macro pattern analysis, refer to my books *Trading Secrets* and *Charting Secrets*.)

Being intrinsically motivated means developing expertise in the nuances of investing and cultivating a resilient mindset so you can navigate both the challenges and the triumphs of the market. You won't rely solely on the emotional highs of profitable trades or market rewards. Your motivation is multifaceted, extending beyond financial gains.

The saying 'money flees need' underscores the importance of setting intrinsic goals. If your focus is solely on extrinsic goals tied to your performance, you're less likely to persevere and find true satisfaction in your results. Intrinsic motivation provides a deeper sense of purpose and fulfilment.

What do you prize or treasure in life?

What would you be willing to fight to protect?

These principles will drive you further than the vanilla goals that so many people write down unenthusiastically.

Motivation waning?

Sharon, a member of my mentor program, asked, 'A year ago I made a loss in the markets. I just can't seem to motivate myself to trade again. What's going on?'

I know some losses can hit you harder than others, so I do hear where Sharon was coming from. I asked her to examine her thoughts in these three areas:

1. Personalisation

If you say to yourself, 'I'm such a klutz, I'm not surprised I'm a failure at trading,' you're blaming yourself for the negative event at a very deep level because of who you are.

The trade and loss isn't *who you are*. It's not a part of you.

Sure, it's good to take responsibility for your actions, but if you personalise it so it's tied in with your sense of identity, then that's a problem.

2. Pervasiveness

If you've ever thought, 'It's not just this loss — I fail at everything!', you have to break free of this thought pattern. A loss in the markets doesn't contaminate every area of your life.

3. Permanence

If you persuade yourself, 'I'll never get this right, I'll never learn how to trade well,' your thoughts are binding you in 'blame land'. Banish the word 'never'.

As traders we have to deal with failure. A lot. Don't let those losses lead to mindset traps that can stop you from taking the next trade.

Change the way you think about your loss, and set mastery goals, and you'll regain your motivation.

What happened to Allyson Felix?

So what happened with Allyson Felix? Did she learn about the disadvantages of the avoidance goal method?

Yes, she did. She went on to become a seven-time Olympic champion, and a *14*-time world champion. She harnessed the power of approach goal setting and visualisation. She says it's about '... quieting my mind, closing my eyes, and really going through the motions of what the perfect race looks like. I ask myself, "What is the perfect race? How did things come together?" Every four years, I have this opportunity—for only about 21 seconds—to get it right.'

That's not to say she didn't face her own challenges. What awaited Felix was more to do with a societal barrier than winning a gold medal.

Felix was used to intensive training six days a week, five hours a day. One of her biggest fears came true in 2018. At six months pregnant, she trained in the dark because she was worried her sponsor would find out about her pregnancy.

Getting pregnant as a competitor in the track and field arena is considered a career-ending 'kiss of death'.

Many athletes are forced to choose between their athletic careers and motherhood. Many sponsorship brands were encouraging women to 'have it all', but apparently that 'all' did not include being a mother. In a very public way, Allyson Felix called out the difficulties for female athletes aiming to have a family.

Felix's legacy is that she totally changed the way sponsors contract their talent. She called out Nike's maternity policy publicly. Now Nike offers 18 months' maternity protection. Other sponsors followed suit and now look after their athletes by protecting pregnancy and child raising contractually.

One year after giving birth, Felix went back to the field and won a gold and a bronze medal. She ultimately became the most decorated woman in Olympic track and field history — all while her daughter was watching. Before becoming a mother she ran for a heap of different reasons. Now she also ran to support women in their choices in life and to encourage them that they can achieve at world-class level after having a child.

So the next time you set goals for yourself in the market, consider how you frame those goals.

As you learn to fly in the markets, don't try to avoid the ground or reach for the stars. Aim to master the task at hand by setting mastery goals. That's where the true rewards lie.

Key concepts

- Goal framing: How we frame our goals — whether as approach goals (striving for positive outcomes) or avoidance goals (avoiding negative outcomes) — can impact our motivation and post-achievement emotions.

- Mastery goals: Mastery goals involve aiming for deep understanding and expertise in a subject. Setting mastery goals can provide greater intrinsic motivation and a sense of purpose on the investing journey.

- Mindset traps: Avoid personalising failures or believing failure is permanent. Overcoming mindset traps can help regain motivation after losses in the markets.

- When setting goals, aim to master the task at hand and find intrinsic motivation in a fascination with the markets. The true rewards lie in mastering the process and growing as a trader.

This next part of the book is the most fun part. It's a series of short stories and exercises to help cement everything we've talked about in the book so far.

KEY 6
Prime your mind for success

Stories and exercises
to reprogram your subconscious

We're so affected by the stories we hear as well as the stories we tell ourselves. When I got serious about trading effectively, I became purposeful about what I read at night. The things you're exposed to first thing in the day and last thing at night have the most impact on your mindset—it's called the primacy and recency effect. That's why I've put together a collection of short stories and exercises for you to turn to any time you need a lift, but ideally before you go to sleep. You can prime your mind for success... and it starts here.

These stories and exercises have the power to directly impact your behaviour in the markets. I know you'll love them. For more fresh morsels of mindset goodness, register on my website to receive my free monthly Trading Game newsletter. Get that done now by going to www.tradinggame.com.au and filling in your details.

CHAPTER 22
Don't delay

What excuses are you feeding yourself? At the end of your days, are you going to tell yourself that you couldn't become a top trader because you couldn't get a babysitter? Or because your boss wouldn't support you?

Allow yourself to get selfish about your goals, because if you don't I'll bet you'll be working to achieve someone else's dreams rather than your own. Say 'no' to anything that doesn't fit in with your plans to be a trader. Adopt a single-minded focus. You'll get what you really want only by pursuing what you really want.

It's tempting to tell ourselves it's okay to wait as the market will always be there. We make excuses for not taking the next trade. But let's face it, if you sit on the sidelines for too long, you may just miss out on the opportunity to double your equity. Benjamin Franklin said, 'He that is good for making excuses is seldom good for anything else.'

A friend of mine is a world-class netball coach. Karen told me once, 'Netball is a long game. Each game tends to form a pattern. To the casual fan, it looks like it's the last five minutes that really count and it's in those precious minutes that the game is won or lost. In reality, though, the only shot the player has is *this* shot, regardless of whether it's at the very start or the very end of the game. If a player starts thinking that a specific shot doesn't matter "in the bigger scheme of things" and there's plenty of time to catch up, they'll soon find themselves taken out of the game.'

Every shot at a trade matters.

If you start thinking, it's okay to miss a trade or two, you'll soon find yourself out of the game. It's *your job* to take each and every signal as they are generated by the market.

People say, 'Que sera sera' or 'Take it easy' or 'You can't win 'em all' or 'It's okay—tomorrow's another day'.

Who says these things?

Poor people, that's who.

Poor people and bad traders.

CHAPTER 23

Should you compare yourself to others?

Fear of missing out (FOMO) is taking over our culture. There are so many people showing their highlight reel on social media while you're going through the grind. It's hard not to compare yourself with others unfavourably. The bright, shiny example of their life may be leading you to think you're coming up short.

Before you go to sleep tonight, ask yourself, *Did I do my best work today?* Once you can answer 'Yes!' without hesitation, it won't matter what others are doing in their lives.

It won't matter if they're on holiday, while you're huddled over your computer working on your trading plan. It won't matter if their children are so witty and clever they'd put Einstein to shame.

All that will matter to you is that you're living your best life.

So should we compare ourselves with others? Here's my controversial answer: 'Hell, yes!'

We need to look outside ourselves to be inspired. But be careful how you do it.

Do this:

- I compare myself in terms of vision and inspiration. There's an osmosis effect here. I can learn about the big thoughts of others, then have big thoughts of my own.

- I compare techniques with a limited group of successful traders. Some things work in the markets, some don't. Keeping the graduates of my mentor program close, as peers, fellow traders in the same ditch ready to fight our way out... well, that's productive. They've tried things I haven't, and many of them have helped me develop short cuts.

Don't do this:

- Don't compare yourself in terms of popularity. The person with loads of friends may not experience intimacy with many or any of them.

- Don't worry about other people's material assets — the car, the house, the boat. These are useless sources of comparison. What does 'success' look like for you? What you're seeing in others is the outward manifestation of what they believe success looks like for them.

Here's the obnoxious truth. You have to believe in your own superiority.

Yes, it sounds like something all the kids in the school yard would laugh at you for. But let's face facts. Unless you put your needs above those of others, and fight for your own place at the table, no one is going to hand it to you on a platter. Andrew Carnegie said the secret to power and wealth was privately to see yourself as superior to others.

This is how hugely successful investors operate. They're sure of themselves, but they're never certain they know it all. They're confident in their abilities, but not sure a specific trade will come out a winner.

You can be confident and cautious at the same time. But if you are *certain* that everything you touch will turn to gold, you abandon all caution, and that makes you a loose cannon.

I wish you confidence, based on the fact that you know you're educating yourself about the financial markets. And with that confidence... yes, I hope you know you're worth it, and you're just a little better than the whinging, whining, snowflake couch potatoes who refuse to lift a finger to help themselves.

Don't replay your past failings and times when the markets got the better of you. Stay away from remorse and pain, or that pain might just put down roots and become permanent. And if it does become permanent, you'll end up associating your trading activities with torment.

Before you trade, replay some of your past successes in your mind. Revel in the feelings of accomplishment this produces. Recognise you are a powerful individual with the ability to control your own destiny.

The markets are your solution. Act like it. Implant those thoughts in your mind before you dare to venture forth into the choppy waters again...

You become what you focus on.

CHAPTER 24

Silver boxes

When I was in my twenties, my grandmother was still very much a part of my life. We both read a book called *Silver Boxes* by Florence Littauer. It spoke of the importance of giving compliments, and providing little silver boxes of appreciation to those you love.

Years later, when Gran was critically ill, we all knew she was facing her very last birthday on this planet. I asked Gran what she'd like for her birthday. Her reply? 'A silver box of love.' Material things had ceased to be important, and all that remained for her was the importance of love.

My family and I bought a beautiful Japanese lacquered box, and we filled it with scrolls describing our love for her.

Knowing you've got limited time with someone makes you cherish them all the more.

Here's a short clip from my message to Gran:

> *How do I express everything you mean to me? It is impossible to encapsulate it in this short scroll. You have provided a foundation of love that guides me through life and keeps me grounded. Tolerance, acceptance and faith. Good humour,*

loyalty and imagination. When I am feeling pressured and stressed I turn to you. You are my role model. The problems of my life melt away under your gentle counsel.

I am me because you have molded my life.

Who in your life needs a compliment... or a few words of appreciation?

We never know how long we have in this life, or what a gift of appreciation — a silver box of love — will do for a person we care about.

I am reminded of Kahlil Gibran's 'On Children' in *The Prophet*. Do you know it? It brings tears to my eyes whenever I read it and recognise its deep resonance of truth.

And a woman who held a babe against her bosom said, 'Speak to us of Children.'

And he said:

Your children are not your children.

They are the sons and daughters of Life's longing for itself.

They come through you but not from you,

And though they are with you, yet they belong not to you.

You may give them your love but not your thoughts.

For they have their own thoughts.

You may house their bodies but not their souls,

For their souls dwell in the house of tomorrow, which you cannot visit, not even in your dreams.

You may strive to be like them, but seek not to make them like you.

For life goes not backward nor tarries with yesterday.

You are the bows from which your children as living arrows are sent forth.

The archer sees the mark upon the path of the infinite, and He bends you with His might that His arrows may go swift and far.

Let your bending in the archer's hand be for gladness;

For even as he loves the arrow that flies, so He loves also the bow that is stable.

I hope this has warmed your trader's heart.

If you have someone who would benefit from a kind word, maybe you could take the leap and send them a message that tells them they're cared for. If you've got a trading buddy, give them this book as a present. I'm sure it would touch them deeply.

CHAPTER 25

Your number one enemy

What is the number one enemy that stops you from investing effectively?

Is it the feeling that you don't have the skills, resources or time to make a bonanza in the markets? Could it be you wonder whether you can hack it?

Well, these self-doubts are hard to overcome, but I can tell you you're facing one even bigger obstacle. Something sinister and totally debilitating. A toxic limb, and if you don't hack it off you'll be lost in the trading wilderness eating bugs for sustenance forever.

This enemy of your success can paralyse you, take away your power and cripple your results.

('Oh come on Louise, just say what the $#^% enemy is already!')

The number one enemy to your growth as a trader can be summed up in two words:

'I KNOW.'

When your mind is full, you won't take in any more information. You'll be crippled, blocking out the essence of genius that is cast in front of you.

I've seen it first-hand, with traders who are sitting in a stink hole of stagnation, wondering why they can't move on.

Maybe you've seen it too?

But when you replace 'I know' with 'Tell me more', you become a sponge ready to absorb information. An empty cup waiting to be filled.

Try it. It might just help you to unlock your ankle cuff and turn a corner in your investment business.

CHAPTER 26

Stumbling blocks

You know what I mean by a stumbling block, don't you? It's one of those insidious investing habits you've adopted that block you from the money the markets offer. Anything that blocks you from money must be abolished.

Which of these stumbling blocks do you suffer from?

1. Trading apnoea (okay, I made that term up). But have you noticed your breathing patterns when you trade? Do you hold your breath when you put a trade on? Many investors do, until they are made aware of the problem. Breathe... heck, just breathe!

2. Do you show your current trades to others? This is called 'talking your book' and is a big 'no-no' in the markets. It invites ego to step in and justify your positions. The markets should be the only thing responsible for telling you whether your analysis is correct... not the opinion of your well-meaning friend.

3. Have you been examining your short-list of the trades you *didn't* take? This is a rare practice, but a very productive one. Watch the progress of the ones you didn't choose. If you had taken them, would they have been profitable? If so, then try to spot the similarities between them. You may have just discovered a brand-new entry trigger.

It's a fact. Identify your stumbling blocks, and you'll trip up far less often.

CHAPTER 27

What's your currency?

'Oh Louise, you don't understand the plight of being a beautiful woman.' She closed her exquisite eyes and two delicate tears rolled down her cheeks.

Beautiful ex-model Lisa had come to me for sharemarket training... or so I thought. In reality she wanted me to rescue her. She'd lost $650K of her pilot husband's superannuation money and she wanted me to dig her out of the hole. With only $140K of her super fund remaining, she'd grown desperate.

Lisa told me how she wanted to be seen as something other than just a pretty trophy. That's why she'd started investing — to prove her worth. But with no training and no mentoring, her descent was fast and hard.

The markets never reward desperation. They only reward clear thinking, discipline and courage. The mirror of the markets reflected Lisa's lack of preparation as a trader.

Lisa's primary 'currency' was her looks.

What's your currency? What do you bring to the world that opens doors, money vaults and opportunities?

If it's something as superficial as your 'looks', you're in trouble... if not today, then tomorrow.

If it's your job title, even that is temporary in these days of rapid retrenchments.

True confidence is based on a currency that doesn't age and that represents your highest values. If you can define your currency, it will grant you rock-solid confidence.

What is *my* currency? I'm glad you asked.

I am the rainmaker. I find hidden pockets of money overlooked by others. It's the currency of all top traders.

We wear our 'rainmaker' badge of honour over our heart. It's a badge we awarded ourselves. A badge no one can take away.

So what happened to that delicate, sad trader who wiped out her husband's retirement money? She didn't grow. She just looked for a quick fix, and an easy solution to a complex problem. Her marriage dissolved, and to this day she continues to hunt for a Prince Charming using the depreciating currency of her beauty.

I predict that unless she changes her currency or backs it up with hard work, she'll never experience happiness. Not every Disney princess ends up living happily ever after.

Define your currency—your worth to the world—and it will set you free.

CHAPTER 28

Can money buy you happiness?

Hell yes... well, yes and no.

Let me explain in seven points:

1. Money can help you strengthen social bonds. You can buy cool things for those you love, to make them feel special and valued.

2. Money can make your relationship conflicts vanish. Fighting about housework? Hire a housekeeper. Annoyed your spouse hasn't cleaned the windows? Stop grizzling and pay your way out of this situation.

3. Exercise costs. One of the best ways to boost your happiness is through exercise. Many of us, however, require gym memberships, costly snow skis and helicopters to drop us off on top of the Alps to really enjoy ourselves. Well, maybe not the helicopter.

4. Experiences last. Once our basic needs are covered, buying great experiences can help us become much happier with life and create brilliant memories too.

5. Security. Money helps buy peace of mind, security for the future and serenity, so financial woes simply vanish.

6. Healthy food often costs more than fast food. But, as we know, eating healthily brings us happiness and long-term benefits.

7. You can spend money on someone else. Whether you support your favourite charity or your niece's education, it's a great feeling to know you've made a difference in someone's life.

Don't discount the importance of money in your life. It can have an impact.

CHAPTER 29
Is this all there is?

Wake up, go to work, come home, go to sleep.

Wake up, go to work, come home, go to sleep.

Wake up, go to work, come home, go to sleep.

Wake up, go to work, come home, go to sleep.

Wake up, go to work, come home, go to sleep.

Wake up, go to work, come home, go to sleep.

Wake up, go to work, come home, go to sleep.

That is the sum total of many people's week. But I know you're not one of the herd.

What are you doing that's different from the majority? It's only by stepping away from the majority that you get to live your own life.

Many of us get so busy making a living we forget we need to make a life. Our busy work is not our life's work.

Surely there's more to life than this and your current situation is not your final destination. Sometimes it takes negotiating the most uncomfortable path to lead you to the greatest pinnacle and the most superb view.

Sometimes it takes a storm to rejuvenate the earth and release the fertility of the soil. And the pain you're feeling will become power. Everything you're now going through will eventually turn into everything you've been through. You'll be looking back on this in days to come, and you'll know it has given you strength and perspective.

Keep looking at your charts, one chart at a time. You can't eat the fruit the same day you plant the seed. The market rewards the patient and punishes the impatient. It takes time.

You will figure this thing out.

It's all there waiting for you.

CHAPTER 30

The self-startler

Years ago, while dating, I encountered a particularly charming creature. He was absolutely fascinating and charismatic. From the moment our eyes met across a crowded room, I was captivated.

Things moved quickly. Over the next few days he showered me with so much attention and affection it left me spinning. Here, it seemed, was someone who truly understood me, who might even be 'the one'. (I had reached this conclusion within a couple of weeks of meeting him.) It all happened very fast. My usual safety mechanisms reserved for the dating game never came close to functioning. I was swept up in his vortex.

Then, as suddenly as it had started, there was a deafening silence. Despite my best efforts to contact him, I didn't hear a thing. No more phone calls, no more letters or cards in the mail, no flower deliveries. After a week of this silence, I received a note that read: 'Won't be able to see you for a while. Need to put the brakes on. Take care. We might catch up in the future.'

What in the heck happened there? Well, I believe he freaked himself out. In a moment of clarity, his happy-go-lucky bachelor subconscious screamed at him, 'Back off mate! At this rate she'll be thinking about picket fences by next month!' So, realising he was in too deep, he decided to run like a frightened rabbit. Like a symmetrical triangle on a chart, things could have gone either way. Either the sky was the limit for the relationship, or he needed to dump me — straight away.

I've seen many self-startler types begin investing. They start with a whirlwind of activity, attend exciting courses, read all the trading books they can get their hands on and generally throw themselves into a love affair with the market. To begin with, they open as many trades as they possibly can and leverage themselves up to the hilt. They tell everyone they will soon retire from their job, become a self-made millionaire and live a life of comfort, because they are on the brink of becoming the next market wizard.

This can now go one of two ways. The self-startler trader can end up resembling a bullish channel and go on to steady investing greatness. It's possible that they'll learn the secrets of effective trading, calm their manic learning curve and develop a steadily profitable, predictable trading plan. Alternatively, as I have seen so many times in the past, they will throw a proverbial top reversal pattern, burn themselves out and blow up their accounts in a blaze of glory. Brief, spectacular and generally downright terrifying to watch.

The symptoms of a potential self-startler can be very disturbing to loved ones. I was recently sent an email by the wife of a new trader that stated simply, 'Help me! I don't even know my husband any more. He's discovered trading, and this is much more attractive to him than I will ever be. He's up half the night trading the US market and has quit his job to trade the Australian market. What can I do?'

Living with someone who is walking the razor's edge is never a pleasant experience.

Finding success in the financial markets is a terrific goal, but it is worthless if the rest of your life is in a shambles. The most successful people in any endeavour tend to have a high level of self-awareness. This is true of profitable traders as well. Most good traders have achieved a level of balance in their lives. They value their health, their personal relationships and often their spiritual life too.

Reading between the lines in Jack Schwager's *Market Wizards*, most superior traders have found a healthy balance in their lives. Occasionally an obsessed, power-hungry person will become a good trader, but such people are the exception rather than the rule.

Initially, you may find that learning about trading occupies your every waking moment, but over time this problem should dissipate. Outstanding traders spend time taking their dog for a walk in the park, they volunteer for tuck-shop duty at their kids' school and they often help their community by giving money to charity. They look after their health and their families, as well as their wealth. Developing mastery over your own mindset and maintaining a balance in your life contribute as much to your trading success as developing appropriate investing strategies.

CHAPTER 31

Your investing identity

I sat beside my grandmother in the retirement village, looking into her dresser mirror. 'Who do you see, Gran?' I asked.

'I see an old woman. I'm always shocked when I see her. Inside I'm still 18 years old, dancing and laughing with my fiancé, my whole life ahead of me.'

Our bodies age, but our minds are so often trapped in the memories of our younger selves. Our youthful abilities are cruelly snatched from us with the passing of the years.

As an investor, once you know how to trade, no one and nothing can sweep aside your skill, and it's something you can do no matter how old you are.

At some stage in our lives we reach our 'invisible midday', when our future days start to be curbed by restrictions. A compression of skills, opportunities and abilities. A tipping point when life ceases to open up, imperceptible at first but growing in intensity with each passing year.

As a trader, though, your midday is indefinitely extended. The skills you learn as a trader carry you into old age, sustaining an intellectual fascination, occupying your mind in a way other retirees cease to experience.

Trading can be your future — and it's a bright one — no matter what your age, gender, culture or background.

You can continue to pick up sparkling gems from the black velvet of the markets, illuminated by your skill and passion.

You, my friend, are a trader... and you always will be.

CHAPTER 32

Eight things I wish people had told me about being a trader

1. **Not everyone will be happy for you.**

    The tall poppy syndrome is alive and well, so be careful
    how you share your dreams, especially early on in your
    investing career. When a dream is first born, it's as fragile
    as a baby bird taking its first flight.

2. **Trading sounds glamorous, but it isn't.**

    The highest performers follow the same routines, day
    in and day out. It's less *Wolf of Wall Street* and more
    Groundhog Day.

3. **People will ask for your latest tip.**

    Never mind the discipline required to develop your short
    list of buys. Disregard the fact most won't be the winners
    you were hoping they'd be. Your friends just want to

know the name of the share that is going to the moon on a one-way trip — and they feel sure you know, but won't tell them.

4. **Your friends and family will think you're unemployed.**

   Full-time traders look like they don't have jobs, so they're asked the most unreasonable favours. Can you drive my son into the city on Wednesday at 4.30 pm? Goodness me! How can you convey that, though you may not look like you're working, *you are working*?

5. **Strangers will think you're a gambler.**

   You'll be expected to agree with fallacies about trading dreamed up by people who have zero knowledge of what you actually do. 'But investing is like gambling, isn't it?' 'You have to be really lucky to get a big win.' 'My neighbour's cousin bet $50 000 on [random crypto] when it was $1.00.' You will be subjected to a torrent of these STUPID comments. Be ready!

6. **You'll be wrong more times than you imagined possible (but still make heaps of money).**

   The greatest trading group in the world, The Turtles, wins only 35 per cent of the time, yet they have amassed a fortune. It's how much money you make each time you win (while keeping your losses small) that counts.

7. **Fellow traders may become your next friendship group.**

   When I started as an investor, I had no idea I'd have so much in common with such a diverse group of like-minded people, all striving to perfect a high-performance endeavour.

8. **'Civilians' will think you're mad.**

Non-traders will never really relate to the calculated risks we take or the way we choose to live our lives. They'll never make the decisions we make to excel and live life on our own terms.

CHAPTER 33

The forgotten struggle

I remember walking to the shop by myself for the first time, pigtails swinging. At four years old, it was a big deal. A huge deal. The lure of a ten-cent bag of lollies sang loudly. How exciting!

Yes, I looked both ways before I crossed the road. And yes, I remembered to turn right at that street with the big tree. Then... disaster struck.

I checked my pocket and it wasn't there. My ten-cent coin had disappeared. Panic set in. With a mournful, strangled cry, I hunted through my clothes. Trying to stay calm, I was choked by tears. Then, just as I had begun to give up hope, our neighbour appeared out of nowhere. With his help I retraced my steps... and voila! The coin was found.

Such relief.

I held onto the coin so tightly as I ran it left an imprint on my palm by the time I got to the milk bar. Those lollies tasted super sweet that day.

Think back over your life. I'll bet many of the things you handle with ease now were once incredibly perplexing. And if that's the case, don't you think that maybe some of the things that seem hard now could seem easy in the future?

What was once a struggle is now a breeze. The struggle is often forgotten once you have conquered a new skill.

The work you're putting in now to learn about investing will set you up for the future. You can pay now, or pay later, but if you pay later … the price will always be higher.

So don't give up. Work on your own education about the markets. Your future you deserves it.

CHAPTER 34

The brutal reality of investing: why honesty is the key

What's one of the toughest challenges most investors face in the markets? It's simple, yet so many fall into the trap that can wreak havoc on their profitability — and their mental health.

What is it?

It's not being honest with yourself.

Having worked in the financial industry for over 30 years, I've seen it all. Investors who hit it big one day only to lose it all the next. Sometimes fools make a killing, while smart and experienced traders struggle to make ends meet. Think about the low-quality stocks or shady schemes that attract crowds, while solid investments with good potential are ignored and neglected.

It's a strange world out there, but staying true to your principles and remaining disciplined will help you navigate it.

Every investing journey has its ups and downs, with the possibility of triumph or failure at every turn. But here's the thing: when things go wrong it's usually because investors aren't being honest with themselves.

They overestimate their skills and make excuses for their failures, only to be shocked when things don't go according to plan. It's tough to face the cold, hard truth that you may be out of sync with the markets, or lack discipline.

Successful traders know taking your ego out of the equation is essential to good decision making. Each individual trade you make is not a reflection of your entire career as an investor. The best investors understand long-term prosperity is built on a foundation of small failures and honest self-reflection.

This is an adventure, full of surprises and unexpected twists and turns. But by being honest with yourself and about your approach, you can navigate the adventure with your sanity intact—and come out on top.

CHAPTER 35
No mud, no lotus

The lotus flower begins life at the bottom of a pond or marsh. This water lily sends roots down into the mud and then pushes its way to the surface through the murky depths. When it surfaces, it unfurls its petals, and its colours shimmer in the sunlight.

Just as the lotus must push through the muddy darkness before it can display its beauty, we must struggle if we are to grow and flourish. It's hard even to imagine the sunlight when we're in the mud. But hope in the face of adversity can lead to wisdom. Beyond the murky darkness, there will be joy and opportunity and comfort.

The lessons you're learning about yourself and the markets will set you up for greatness in the future, if you pay attention. It's hard to move through suffering with grace and courage. When you're on high alert, your focus may narrow until all you can see is how to protect yourself and your immediate family. I get it. But when we try to evade suffering, we only prolong and intensify it.

These conflicting emotions are natural. Instead of running away, learn to gently be with your pain. Hold it tenderly. Feel it. When your mind is still, pain can lead to transformation and growth. No mud, no lotus.

The traders who decide to enjoy the process and the lessons they learn while pursuing trading excellence are the ones who come out on top. Choose to enjoy the pressure and discomfort of learning new strategies. But if you think that one day the pain will be over, think again.

Pain means you're growing. If you're 100 per cent comfortable, you have reached your summit — it's all downhill from there.

CHAPTER 36

Cane toad narcotics

My fur-nephew is a plucky little sausage dog called Wilfred. His hobby? Hunting cane toads.

Once he catches one, he rolls it on its side. Then he gently squashes it with his paw and delightedly licks the oozing yellow poison it secretes from its slimy glands. Wilfred then gets an immediate hallucinogenic high, and wins an emergency trip to the vet to have his stomach pumped.

Time and time again.

Bizarre behaviour even for a dog. Does he learn from these multiple traumas? Apparently not. This is the power of addiction.

How do you know whether you're a cool, collected, logical trader or simply addicted to the market action?

Here's how to tell. Ask yourself these yes or no questions:

1. Is it more important for you to trade than to be profitable?

2. Do you live for the high of the win, rather than aiming for emotional detachment?

3. Do you go on gut feel, rather than following a carefully conceived trading plan?

4. Do you refuse to accept the help of an experienced mentor, because you think you know it all?

5. Do you look at your own positions constantly, rather than allowing yourself some much-needed downtime?

Let's see how you went. Count up your 'yes' answers.

0-1: You are in control, not addicted to the market action. You're doing what it takes to trade successfully. If you're not yet profitable, it's only a matter of time.

2-3: You do have some risk of addiction. Beware, because the equivalent of a stomach pump at the vet will be your fate if you don't address this issue.

4-5: You are in full-blown cane toad addiction to the markets. Stop what you're doing immediately and check yourself into investing rehab with a mentor today. Re-read this book and make sure you implement evidence-based methods to get your investing on track.

CHAPTER 37

Investing lessons from Cleo the cat

Have you ever watched a cat stalk a bird?

I secretly fed my neighbour's cat, Cleo, when I was a child. She taught me some valuable lessons about trading.

Cleo was a pro when it came to stalking. Sweet little Cleo sees the sparrow *and immediately switches to murder mode.*

She isn't playing with a ball of wool anymore. No. Now she's *serious.* She zeroes in on her target. Every muscle is taut.

She inches closer, holding a pose for minutes at a time. We're talking Zen patience here, every fibre of her being is focused on taking down her prey.

Finally… *she pounces.*

The bell around her neck means she doesn't ever succeed, but she doesn't freak out. She returns to her hidey-spot and waits for the next opportunity. I remember watching Cleo work. (Admittedly, after she savaged my arm, I kept my distance and spied on her from my vantage point high up in my tree house.)

What I learned from her is relevant to *trading*.

- Veterans don't rush into every opportunity. No way. They *stalk* it first.

- The exceptional trader stays loyal to what worked in the past — stealth, patience and then speed — in that order.

- Sometimes, even when you're doing everything right (like feeding Cleo), the markets can be savage, and you have to know when to step back.

- Even more relevant: exceptional investors gauge their own skills against what is necessary to win.

Rookies become overexcited about getting into, say, the two-minute FX market. They hear how much money there is to be made and can't wait to dive in.

Of course, they quickly discover that while it's easy to get into that murky pool, if you don't know what you're doing, you'll sink.

The first advice I give anyone looking at a new market is simply to *study* it first.

That's what the pros do.

CHAPTER 38

Love affair with money

People's love affair with money has always fascinated me. Want to see normal people do completely bizarre things? Add money and let the games begin.

How about the friend who disappears after you lend him money? What's going on there? Or the siblings who create merry hell at the reading of their father's will? Or the bloke with the secret bank account that he isn't telling his wife about? And then there's the girl who spends too much to impress people she doesn't like with money she doesn't have?

Money can make ordinary people behave very badly! Is money itself bad? Of course not. What the heck happens in situations like this?

Money, in and of itself, is neutral, until we empower it, giving it meaning. It's our own thoughts and emotions around money that determine whether it's a positive or negative force in our lives.

I guarantee this: change your thinking about money and what it means to you, and you'll change your results as a trader.

Once we realise that money is nothing more than a tool, we refuse its power over us. We stop it from controlling our thoughts and our actions. Ironically, this knowledge paves the way for more of it to enter our lives.

So which comes first? Attitudes about money, or money itself?

Having trained hundreds of successful traders, and seen them at every stage of their wealth development, I can definitely answer this one. The attitude towards money comes first. The way a trader thinks always precedes their actual share trading results.

CHAPTER 39

How an exotic dancer changed the way I viewed investing forever

While we can learn a lot from our fellow traders, there is also a wealth of valuable information we can derive from other sources. I'm a firm believer in borrowing from other people's experience to derive essential lessons I can apply to my own life. Let's have a look at the life of one the more colourful characters in show business history, Ms Lola Montez.

Born Eliza Gilbert in Ireland in 1821, she came to Paris in the 1840s dreaming of hitting the big time as a dancer and actress. She changed her name to the exotic Lola Montez, and set about using her feminine wiles to woo some incredibly influential men. First on the scoreboard was Alexandre Dujarier, owner of the newspaper with the largest circulation in France at that time. Dujarier's life and business dealings began to slide downhill almost overnight. When a champion pistol shooter insulted Lola at a party, Dujarier unwisely challenged him to a duel. (You know nothing good can come of this, don't you?) Dujarier was shot dead the next day.

Lola moved to Munich and set her sights on King Ludwig of Bavaria. In his own words, he became 'bewitched' by Lola and, ignoring his counsellors, took her as his mistress. The Bavarians loved their king but they hated Lola. When civil war broke out in 1848 Ludwig was forced to abdicate and Lola fled.

In the interests of brevity, I will briefly summarise the next few years of Lola's life. She moved to England, wrecked another bloke's career. She promptly married another guy, who became depressed and died within a couple of years. Oh yeah…and somewhere along the way, she ended up being charged with bigamy. Crikey!

Now what possible investing lesson can we derive from this sorry tale?

Well, one is we become like those with whom we associate, so unless you're set on becoming a bigamist, and bringing death and ruin to all around you, be sure to associate with people who are positive, encouraging and uplifting.

Some people seem to attract chaos and disaster, no matter what their circumstances. If you befriend these types of people, you will soon become infected. As a trader, you'll likely fall into a whirlpool of self-doubt about your abilities. If you feel pity for a fellow trader, take it as a warning that you yourself are nanoseconds away from being sucked into their mire of bad luck and self-defeating patterns of behaviour. Associate with successful traders who have your best interests at heart.

The other lesson I believe we can learn from Lola is that our circumstances can do a v-reversal very suddenly. When the world comes crashing down around us, a change of fortune may wait just around the corner that can lead us to riches beyond our imaginings. Be grateful when things are on the up and up, but don't take success for granted, as you may be just a stone's throw from one of life's humbling experiences.

CHAPTER 40

Are you a dandelion or an orchid trader?

There is a theory that some children are born dandelions. No matter the terrain, no matter how much or how little sunlight and water they receive, they will thrive. Dandelion children are typically sociable and extroverted. They are what psychologists term low-reactives.

High-reactive children are like orchids — they don't thrive just anywhere, but under the right conditions, they prove to be both strong and awe-inspiring. Jay Belsky, a psychology professor from the University of London, explains that high-reactive kids can be overwhelmed by childhood adversity. They are at risk of depression, anxiety, and shyness, for instance, in a stressful family environment.

However, recent research suggests high-reactives benefit more from a supportive, nurturing environment than do low-reactives. In other words, high-reactive children are more strongly affected by positive as well as by negative experiences. The strengths and the sensitivities come as a package deal.

High-reactive children who enjoy good parenting, child care and stability actually experience fewer emotional problems in adulthood than their low-reactive peers. They are empathic, caring and thoughtful. They become successful at the things that matter to them and often mediate to smooth the troubled waters of group interactions.

What does this have to do with the markets? In my view, there are orchid traders and dandelion traders. Orchid traders take a long time to learn about the markets. They can feel they're behind the eight-ball and wonder whether they'll ever excel. They experience self-doubt and need the support and care of a mentor to bring them through to the next level. They may need to be shown rather than told how to trade. They wilt under criticism but thrive with encouragement. Once they grasp the necessary skills, orchid traders rise to the top and are exceptional. The only risk is that they may not hang in there long enough because they may be overwhelmed by feelings of inadequacy.

Dandelion traders, on the other hand, are quick to learn and tend to excel from the very beginning, no matter the market odds. They weather the storms of criticism as if they were spring showers. However, even though they bloom where they are planted, they often find that because success has come so easily to them, they don't have to strive and focus.

Which kind of trader will you be? The one who experiences easy success, or the one who will have to struggle but will become exceptional?

I reckon we orchids outnumber the dandelions around 30 to 1.

CHAPTER 41

Permission to be rich

No financial condition is permanent unless you give it permission to be so.

I've been through a few wipeouts in my life. I was wiped out emotionally when I didn't get into the university course I aspired to. I had a business in personnel while I was at university that I drove into the ground. I was wiped out emotionally and financially when I invested in the now defunct Pyramid Building Society. Oh yeah... then I was wiped out when I lost the use of my arms for a couple of years, which led me to leave my corporate role to become a full-time trader.

I firmly believed that no financial position I found myself in could become permanent, unless I chose to let it become so. Had I fertilised this belief with negativity, had I allowed it to take root, then it would have flourished and become permanent. I would never have been able to mount another comeback, to re-create myself.

There are no absolute certainties in life. Even as I write this, I hope I'll never have to launch another 'Louise Bedford revival campaign'. I can tell you, rebounding is no fun. However, I hold onto the thought that each recreation has come a little more easily, thanks to the benefit of experience.

What is it you are hanging onto? Is there a life circumstance you've allowed to take root like a noxious weed? Are you planning to create a totally new reality for yourself?

The best traders plan for success long before there are any real signs they can achieve it. In their mind's eye they can see the life they want to lead, the money they want to earn and the people they want to associate with. They don't like setbacks (who does!). But they compartmentalise their current reality so they can work on making the future a reality. They refuse to let the past dictate what will happen in their lives over the next few years.

Right now, you may be neck-deep in problems. You may be stabbed with feelings that you're not worthy of success. You may be picturing a future that doesn't include spreading your wings. I guarantee that if you feed these negative feelings, if you give them permission to take root, they will become a permanent fixture in your life.

No financial situation is permanent, unless you decide it is.

CHAPTER 42

Yes, they saw my undies

I'd just finished presenting to a huge audience. A roar of applause. I glided towards the edge of the stage to make my carefully timed exit.

High heels. Professional. A new, flowing dress. And then, as I stepped down from the stage, I stumbled.

Not a graceful little skip and misstep. No, no, no.

A full missed step. Heavy footed. And down I went. Clunk, clunk, clunk down the four steps leading from the stage, landing on the floor in a crumpled heap of arms and legs.

The audience gave a collective gasp of horror.

'Are you okay?' came the cries of concern. 'Have you hurt yourself?'

I paused. Wiggled my toes. My new dress was flipped up around my waist. Yes, I was okay. Every part of me. Except my ego.

The silence was heavy, my friend. Struck with inspiration — I leapt to my feet, threw my arms in the air and yelled: 'Ta-da!'

Everyone laughed as I gamely staggered off to the back room.

We could see this as a metaphor. The markets are a great training ground. They teach you strength. They teach you resilience. They teach you to think fast and not take yourself too seriously.

Will you fall down as a trader?

Why yes. Yes you will.

But remember, it's not what happens to you as a trader. It's how you handle what happens.

CHAPTER 43

Are you ready to become a full-time trader?

I didn't choose the time to quit my job in 1996. I got laid off.

I'm not the first person this has ever happened to, but I felt as though I was. Walking out of that office block for the last time filled me with shame and guilt as well as frustration. But I also felt a seed of hope as I pictured my life as a full-time trader. Could I do it? What would it involve? What if it didn't work out and I had to go back to a work environment that didn't nurture my higher purpose?

Empty days stretched ahead with little to fill them except charts. I was forced to feel. To slow down. To acknowledge who I was and what was important to me.

Looking back, it's as though there was some sort of master plan but that's not how it felt at the time. It wasn't until later — much later — I could look back and make sense of what had happened.

Sometimes we can't see the script we're following until later. We don't see how the puzzle pieces will fit together.

Sure, I went on to make a good living from the markets. I wrote five best-selling books and travelled the world helping other traders. And my husband and I became full-time parents. However, in the dark hours of day one as a free person, I couldn't know what lay ahead. I was ashamed of leaving my profession and I felt guilty. Had I tried hard enough to succeed in the corporate world?

Before you decide to quit your job, ask yourself a few pertinent questions:

Have you honed the necessary skills to make money regardless of market conditions?

If you do not know how to make money out of markets that trend down and sideways, then you will only make money in a bull market. This is not sustainable over the long haul. It would be horrible to have to go back to work having once made your escape.

Do you have sufficient capital to continue trading should you suffer a string of losses?

Can you build your capital and increase your position size based on your trading results? If you can't add to your equity, inflation will ultimately bite you. Many investors begin their full-time investing career undercapitalised and spend their first few months eating baked beans and recalling the days when money flowed freely and losses didn't matter.

Can you exit a trade when it has turned against you?

If not, you will eventually self-destruct. It's only a matter of time.

Have you been able to bank your primary source of income for at least a year and live solely on your investing income?

If not, the pressure of trading for a living when you quit your 'real' job could adversely affect your decisions in the markets.

Do you have the support of your family?

It's up to you to make sure your family understands your plan for the future and how it will unfold. It will mean a dramatic change for you all once you start trading full-time.

It's just the beginning

I've been a trader practically all my adult life. I started when I was 20. I've traded while I was single and after I married and had children. I've marked my time in the markets alongside the ages of my two daughters.

My children are grown up now. The years have passed in a flash and my babies are spreading *their* wings.

Tall, elegant and contemplative Ramona. At 21 years old, she's finding her way in the world, pursuing her love of mathematics and physics at uni.

Ambitious, enthusiastic and athletic Ash. At 17 years old, she sings with adult clarity. Self-possessed, confident and enchanting, she is ready to conquer the world.

Oh my god, I think, suddenly aware of my thumping heartbeat. They're not little anymore! When did that happen? I can't place it. It seems like I looked away for just a moment, and my babies were gone — just like that.

The trace of their babyhood is only evident now on their sleeping faces, or when they are overcome with laughter, or when they feel vulnerable and need a hug.

The soft preciousness of their early childhood was so fleeting. Their silky soft skin and wispy hair. The way their bodies would collapse into me as they fell asleep. The smell of fresh talcum powder and baby shampoo. The 'firsts' between then and now.

Of course I am no longer their entire world. I feel the wrench of letting them go as they move with lightning speed into adulthood.

They've only ever known a mum and dad who have both been full-time parents, all because of the decision I made years ago to learn how to trade.

Wasn't it just yesterday when they were climbing onto my lap with a sippy cup?

Nothing can prepare you for this.

The days are long, but the years are short.

In some ways, I think of *you* as one of my children as well, and it makes me feel a bit wistful. As a new investor or trader you'll have so many firsts.

Your first complete trading plan.

Your first investment.

First little loss.

First major win.

Plus, down the track as your skill as an investor grows, the first time you realise you've changed the trajectory of your family's lives because of the decision you made to trade.

For more experienced investors, I hope the lessons I've shared with you in this book will help you navigate the pressures of the market. And if you're just starting out, I envy you because this is exactly the mindset guide I would have loved as I struggled to become established in this trading game.

I've seen so many of my investors begin in the markets over the years — wary, nervous, wondering whether they've got what it takes. I've seen them develop their skills and their confidence, drinking in the support I could provide. I've watched them like a mother as they stumble, get back on their feet, and continue to trade, eventually making the markets their home, nimbly changing direction when required, but staying true to their trading plans.

My heart swells with pride as I watch their accomplishments. I see the changes they're making in their lives. The years flash by in the blink of an eye.

I don't take my role as mentor lightly. I treat it with the care and attention it deserves. Helping people excel in the markets has been the biggest passion project of my life.

I'm feeling the passing of the years more keenly than ever. Are you?

Isn't it about time you stopped letting the years gallop past without consciously focusing on your goals? Isn't it time you got this trading game nailed, once and for all?

Take what I've given you and work as hard on your personal development as you do on your trading plan. I want to see you excel in the markets.

You can lean on my shoulder and tell me about the things that feel raw.

The pink places that have been sand-papered by the markets.

Your head, your heart, your pride.

And I will understand, at a deep level, because I have been there. I have experienced the pain of a losing trade and the exhilaration of a winner. I know the grind of following your plan when the markets aren't cooperating. And I also know what it feels like to experience hope for a brighter future.

What's your personal manifesto?

Here's mine — direct from the pages of my morning journal. (Feel free to borrow the parts that appeal to you.)

I create my own safety.

I am my own role model.

I am capable.

I am bold, not mild.

I confront challenges head-on and reap the rewards and confidence this brings.

I am not my past.

Remember the prize. Remember why you're playing this crazy, irritating, rewarding, exciting, delightful trading game.

Go forth loudly and boldly. Open the floodgates to your emancipation. You do yourself no favours by playing small. To waste a life full of potential, to die with your glorious gifts still firmly planted within your body instead of expressed for the world to see, would be a travesty.

One thing is certain: you may flounder and struggle but you will grow. You will spread your wings and soar.

You have made a choice by reading this book. If you chase success, without honouring the six golden keys to psychological fitness, you will fail. However, if you use these keys and continue to refine your methods, success will be a foregone conclusion.

Let your light shine as an investor.

You never know what ripple effect this will create not just in your life, but in the lives of those watching from the sidelines.

Sources

Key 1 intro

Tierney, J 2011, 'Do You Suffer from Decision Fatigue?', *The New York Times*, 17 August.

Wood, W, Quinn, J & Kashy, D 2002, 'Habits in Everyday Life: Thought, Emotion, and Action', *Journal of Personality and Social Psychology*, vol. 83, no. 6.

Chapter 1

Biais, B, Mazurier, K & Pouget, S 2002, 'Psychological Traits and Trading Strategies', *Centre for Economic Policy Research Discussion Paper Series*, vol. 3195.

Cote, C 2022, *Growth Mindset vs. Fixed Mindset: What's the Difference?*, Business Insights blog, viewed 13 December 2023.

Dweck, C 2017, *Mindset: Changing the Way You Think to Fulfill Your Potential*, Robinson, London.

Dweck, CS 2009, 'Mindsets: Developing Talent through a Growth Mindset', *Olympic Coach*, vol. 21, no. 4.

Lo, AW, Repin, DV & Steenbarger, BN 2005, 'Fear and Greed in Financial Markets: A Clinical Study of Day-Traders', *National Bureau of Economic Research*, Working Paper Series, no. 11243.

Schwager, JD 2009, *The New Market Wizards: Conversations with America's top traders*, HarperCollins E-Books, New York.

Sharot, T 2011, 'The Optimism Bias', *Current Biology*, vol. 21, no. 23, pp. R941–5.

Sullivan, MJL, Thorn, B, Haythornthwaite, JA, et al. 2001, 'Theoretical Perspectives on the Relation between Catastrophizing and Pain', *The Clinical Journal of Pain*, vol. 17, no. 1, pp. 52–64.

Chapter 2

Dai, H, Milkman, KL & Riis, J 2014, 'The Fresh Start Effect: Temporal Landmarks Motivate Aspirational Behavior', *Management Science*, vol. 60, no. 10, pp. 2563–82.

Dean, J 2013, *Making Habits, Breaking Habits*, Da Capo Lifelong Books.

Gardner, B & Rebar, AL 2019, 'Habit Formation and Behavior Change', *Oxford Research Encyclopedia of Psychology*, viewed 12 December 2023.

Gardner, B, Lally, P & Wardle, J 2012, 'Making health habitual: the psychology of "habit-formation" and general practice', *British Journal of General Practice*, vol. 62, no. 605, pp. 664–6.

Kruglanski, AW & Szumowska, E 2020, 'Habitual Behavior Is Goal-Driven', *Perspectives on Psychological Science*, vol. 15, no. 5, pp. 1256–71.

Lally, P, van Jaarsveld, CHM, Potts, HWW & Wardle, J 2010, 'How are habits formed: Modelling habit formation in the real world', *European Journal of Social Psychology*, vol. 40, no. 6, pp. 998–1009.

McDermott, L, Dobson, A & Russell, A 2004, 'Changes in smoking behaviour among young women over life stage transitions', *Australian and New Zealand Journal of Public Health*, vol. 28, no. 4, pp. 330-5.

Price, LL, Coulter, RA, Strizhakova, Y & Schultz, AE 2017, 'The Fresh Start Mindset: Transforming Consumers' Lives', in E Fischer & S Shavitt (eds), *Journal of Consumer Research*, vol. 45, no. 1, pp. 21-48.

Rothman, AJ 2000, 'Toward a theory-based analysis of behavioral maintenance', *Health Psychology*, vol. 19, no. 1, Suppl, pp. 64-9.

Tate, C 2013, *Stillness Revisited*, Trading Game, viewed 11 December 2023.

Verplanken, B, Myrbakk, V & Rudi, V 2005, 'The Measurement of Habit', in T Betsch & S Haberstroh (eds), *The Routines of Decision Making*, Lawrence Erlbaum Associates Publishers, pp. 231-47.

Chapter 3

Amaya, KA & Smith, KS 2018, 'Neurobiology of habit formation', *Current Opinion in Behavioral Sciences*, vol. 20, pp. 145-52.

Doidge, N 2007, *The Brain that Changes Itself: Stories of Personal Triumph from the Frontiers of Brain Science*, Scribe, Melbourne.

Sakai, J 2020, 'Core Concept: How synaptic pruning shapes neural wiring during development and, possibly, in disease', *Proceedings of the National Academy of Sciences*, vol. 117, no. 28.

Smith, K & Graybiel, A 2016, 'Habit formation', *Dialogues in Clinical Neuroscience*, vol. 18, no. 1, pp. 33-43.

Chapter 4

Cobb Payton, F & White, SD 2003, 'Views from the field on mentoring and roles of effective networks for minority IT doctoral students', SIGMIS CPR '03: Proceedings of the 2003 SIGMIS conference on Computer personnel research: Freedom in Philadelphia — leveraging differences and diversity in the IT workforce, 10 April.

Dekker, S, Cilliers, P & Hofmeyr, J-H 2011, 'The complexity of failure: Implications of complexity theory for safety investigations', *Safety Science*, vol. 49, no. 6, pp. 939–45.

Jones, RL, Harris, R & Miles, A 2009, 'Mentoring in sports coaching: a review of the literature', *Physical Education & Sport Pedagogy*, vol. 14, no. 3, pp. 267–84.

Kipchumba Tarus, B 2014, 'Mentorship as an Antecedent of High Performance Workplace in Selected Water Boards in Kenya', *European Journal of Business and Management*, vol. 6, no. 21, viewed 12 December 2023.

Toledo-Pereyra, LH 2009, 'Mentoring Surgeons', *Journal of Investigative Surgery*, vol. 22, no. 2, pp. 77–81.

Yirci, R & Kocabaş, İ 2010, 'The Importance of Mentoring for School Principals: A Conceptual Analysis', *International Journal of Educational Leadership Preparation*.

Chapter 5

Lo, AW, Repin, DV & Steenbarger, BN 2005, 'Fear and Greed in Financial Markets: A Clinical Study of Day-Traders', *National Bureau of Economic Research*, Working Paper Series, no. 11243.

Chapter 6

Andrews, S, Ellis, DA, Shaw, H et al. 2015, 'Beyond self-report: Tools to compare estimated and real-world smartphone use', *Plos One*, October 28.

Danziger, S, Levav, J & Avnaim-Pesso, L 2011, 'Extraneous factors in judicial decisions', *PNAS*, vol. 108, no. 17.

Kelly, L, Miller-Ott, AE & Duran, RL 2019, 'Phubbing friends: Understanding face threats from, and responses to, friends' cell phone usage through the lens of politeness theory', *Communication Quarterly*, vol. 67, no. 5.

Kruger, DJ et al. 2017, 'Cell phone use latency in a midwestern USA university population', *Journal of Technology in Behavioral Science*, vol. 2, pp. 56–9.

Lang, SS 2002, 'Study of German children living near airports shows jet aircraft noise impairs long-term memory and reading ability', *Cornell Chronicle*, October 7.

Leland, A et al. 2017, 'The role of dual tasking in the assessment of gait, cognition and community reintegration of veterans with mild traumatic brain injury', National Library of Medicine, *Mater Sociomed.*, vol. 29 no. 4, pp. 251–6.

Mark, G, Gudith, D & Klocke, U 2008, 'The cost of interrupted work: More speed and stress', CHI: Conference on Human Factors in Computing Systems, ACM, April 6.

Peraman, R & Parasuraman, S 2016, 'Mobile phone mania: A rising global threat in public health', *Journal of Natural Science, Biology and Medicine*, vol. 7, no. 2, p. 198.

Sander, L 2023, '"Disastrous experiment": Real reason behind hated return to work push', news.com.au, 8 June, viewed 12 December 2023.

Strayer, DL, Drews, FA & Johnson, WA 2003, *'Are we being driven to distraction?'* Center for Public Policy and Administration, University of Utah, Public Policy Perspectives, vol. 16, pp. 1–2.

Chapter 7

Breggin, PR 2014, *Guilt, Shame, and Anxiety: understanding and overcoming negative emotions*, Prometheus Books, Amherst, New York.

Cox, J & Johnson, J 2022, *Healing from Toxic Shame*, Psych Central, viewed 13 February 2023.

Hansen, M, Amabile, T, Snook, S & Craig, N 2018, *Purpose, Meaning, and Passion*, Harvard Business Review Press, Boston, Massachusetts.

Lefebvre, J-I, Montani, F & Courcy, F 2020, 'Self-Compassion and Resilience at Work: A Practice-Oriented Review', *Advances in Developing Human Resources*, vol. 22, no. 4.

Scheff, T 2000, 'Shame and the social bond: A sociological theory', *Sociological Theory*, vol. 18, pp. 84–99.

Vliet, KJ 2009, 'The role of attributions in the process of overcoming shame: A qualitative analysis', *Psychology and Psychotherapy: Theory, Research and Practice*, vol. 82, no. 2, pp. 137–52.

World of Work Project 2019, *Drowning Rats Psychology Experiment: Resilience and the Power of Hope*, The World of Work Project, viewed 6 December 2021.

Chapter 8

Ashe, ML & Wilson, SJ 2020, 'A brief review of choice bundling: A strategy to reduce delay discounting and bolster self-control', *Addictive Behaviors Reports*, vol. 11.

Binda, DD, Greco, CM & Morone, NE 2022, 'What Are Adverse Events in Mindfulness Meditation?', *Global Advances in Health and Medicine*, vol. 11.

Douglas, MJ 2000, *Trading in the Zone: Master the Market with Confidence, Discipline and a Winning Attitude*, New York Institute of Finance, New York.

Farias, M, Maraldi, E, Wallenkampf, KC & Lucchetti, G 2020, 'Adverse events in meditation practices and meditation-based therapies: a systematic review', *Acta Psychiatrica Scandinavica*, vol. 142, no. 5.

Hsiao, F, Liu, TL, Chien, Y-H, Lee, MT & Hirst, RJ 2006, 'The development of a target-lock-on optical remote sensing system for unmanned aerial vehicles', *Journal of the Royal Aeronautical Society*, vol. 110, Cambridge University Press, no. 1105, pp. 163–72.

Johnson, R & Cureton, A 2004, *Kant's Moral Philosophy*, Stanford Encyclopedia of Philosophy.

Killeen, P, Green, L & Neuringer, A 2021, 'Howard Rachlin (1935–2021)', *American Psychologist*, vol. 76, no. 8, p. 1349.

Newport, C 2016, *Deep Work: Rules for focused success in a distracted world*, Piatkus, London.

Rachlin, H & Siegel, E 1994, 'Temporal Patterning in Probabilistic Choice', *Organizational Behavior and Human Decision Processes*, vol. 59, no. 2, pp. 161–76.

Wiseman, R 2004, *The Luck Factor*, Arrow Books, London.

Chapter 9

Charoensukmongkol, P & Aumeboonsuke, V 2016, 'Does mindfulness enhance stock trading performance?: the moderating and mediating effects of impulse control difficulties', *International Journal of Work Organisation and Emotion*, vol. 7, no. 4, p. 257.

Craske, MG 2010, *Cognitive-behavioral Therapy*, American Psychological Association (APA).

Emmons, RA & Stern, R 2013, 'Gratitude as a Psychotherapeutic Intervention', *Journal of Clinical Psychology*, vol. 69, no. 8, pp. 846–55.

Gilbert, P 1998, 'The evolved basis and adaptive functions of cognitive distortions', *British Journal of Medical Psychology*, vol. 71, no. 4, pp. 447–63.

Wormwood, JB, Siegel, EH, Kopec, J, Quigley, KS & Barrett, LF 2019, 'You are what I feel: A test of the affective realism hypothesis', *Emotion*, vol. 19, no. 5, pp. 788–98.

Chapter 10

Britt-Lutter, S, Haselwood, C & Koochel, E 2018, 'Love and Money: Reducing Stress and Improving Couple Happiness', *Marriage & Family Review*, vol. 55, no. 4, pp. 330–45.

Britt, SL & Huston, SJ 2012, 'The Role of Money Arguments in Marriage', *Journal of Family and Economic Issues*, vol. 33, no. 4, pp. 464–76.

Dew, J, Britt, S & Huston, S 2012, 'Examining the Relationship between Financial Issues and Divorce', *Family Relations*, vol. 61, no. 4, pp. 615–28.

Horwitz, E & Klontz, B 2013, 'Understanding and Dealing with Client Resistance to Change', *Journal of Financial Planning*, November 2013.

Payne, K 2018, *The Broken Ladder: How inequality affects the way we think, live, and die*, Penguin, New York.

Your Mental Wealth Advisors 2020, *Your Money Script*, Your Mental Wealth Advisors, viewed 12 December 2023.

Chapter 11

Barber, BM & Odean, T 1998, 'Boys Will Be Boys: Gender, Overconfidence, and Common Stock Investment', *SSRN Electronic Journal*, vol. 116, no. 1.

Booth, A, Granger, DA, Mazur, A & Kivlighan, KT 2006, 'Testosterone and Social Behavior', *Social Forces*, vol. 85, no. 1, pp. 167–91.

Brockman, K 2023, *Ninety-one percent of women think men are better investors — here's why that couldn't be more wrong*, Fidelity Investments, viewed 12 December 2023.

Canoles, WB, Thompson, S, Irwin, S & France, V 1998, 'An analysis of the profiles and motivations of habitual commodity speculators', *Journal of Futures Markets*, vol. 18, no. 7, pp. 765–801.

Financial Times n.d., *Women trade less often than men, with better results*, viewed 12 December 2023.

Lieber, R 2021, 'Women May Be Better Investors Than Men. Let Me Mansplain Why', *The New York Times*, 29 October, viewed 12 December 2023.

Railey, M 2022, *Op-ed: If female investors have any weakness, it's their mistaken belief that they're not good investors*, CNBC, viewed 21 September 2023.

Semenova, A 2022, *Women portfolio managers are beating their male colleagues in 2022's market drawdown*, Yahoo Finance, viewed 12 December 2023.

Soe, A 2019, *The Financial Future Is Female*, S&P Global, viewed 12 December 2023.

Wieczner, J 2017, 'Women-Run Hedge Funds Are Beating the Rest', Fortune, viewed 12 December 2023.

Chapter 12

Klontz, B & Britt, S 2012, 'How Clients' Money Scripts Predict Their Financial Behaviors', *Journal of Financial Planning*, November 2012, pp. 33–43.

Romo, LK & Vangelisti, AL 2014, 'Money Matters: Children's Perceptions of Parent–Child Financial Disclosure', *Communication Research Reports*, vol. 31, no. 2, pp. 197–209.

Chapter 14

Mathers, L 2022, Curious Habits: Why we do what we do and how to change, Major Street.

Parker, CB 2015, 'Embracing stress is more important than reducing stress, Stanford psychologist says', *Stanford News*, May 7.

Selye, H 1950, 'Stress and the General Adaptation Syndrome', *British Medical Journal*, vol. 1, no. 4667, pp. 1383–92.

Tickell, J 2003, *Laughter, Sex, Vegetables & Fish: 10 Secrets of Long Living People*, Crown Content.

Weisinger, H & Pawliw-Fry, JP 2015, Performing Under Pressure: The science of doing your best when it matters most, Crown Business, New York.

Chapter 15

Bernstein, J 1986, *Beyond the Investors Quotient: The inner world of investing*, Wiley.

Bollu, PC & Kaur, H 2019, 'Sleep Medicine: Insomnia and Sleep', *Missouri Medicine*, vol. 116, *Journal of the Missouri State Medical Association*, no. 1, pp. 68–75.

CDC 2021, *How Does Sleep Affect Your Heart Health?*, Centers for Disease Control and Prevention, viewed 12 December 2023.

Eisenberger, NI 2012, 'Broken Hearts and Broken Bones', *Current Directions in Psychological Science*, vol. 21, no. 1, pp. 42–7.

Guarana, CL, Stevenson, RM, Gish, JJ, Ryu, JW & Crawley, R 2022, 'Owls, larks, or investment sharks? The role of circadian process in early-stage investment decisions', *Journal of Business Venturing*, vol. 37, no. 1.

Loehr, JE & McLaughlin, PJ 1988, *Mentally Tough*, M. Evans.

Pennebaker, JW & Chung, CK 2011, 'Expressive writing: Connections to physical and mental health', in HS Friedman (ed.), *The Oxford Handbook of Health Psychology*, Oxford University Press, pp. 417–37.

Zarse, EM, Neff, MR, Yoder, R et al. 2019, 'The adverse childhood experiences questionnaire: Two decades of research on childhood trauma as a primary cause of adult mental illness, addiction, and medical diseases', in U Schumacher (ed.), *Cogent Medicine*, vol. 6, no. 1.

Chapter 16

Fenton-O'Creevy, M, Lins, JT, Vohra, S et al. 2012, 'Emotion regulation and trader expertise: Heart rate variability on the trading floor', *Journal of Neuroscience, Psychology, and Economics*, vol. 5, no. 4, pp. 227–37.

Gervais, S & Odean, T 1997, 'Learning to Be Overconfident', *SSRN Electronic Journal*.

Hariharan, A, Adam, MTP, Astor, PJ & Weinhardt, C 2015, 'Emotion regulation and behavior in an individual decision trading experiment: Insights from psychophysiology', *Journal of Neuroscience, Psychology, and Economics*, vol. 8, no. 3, pp. 186–202.

Kandasamy, N, Garfinkel, SN, Page, L et al. 2016, 'Interoceptive Ability Predicts Survival on a London Trading Floor', *Scientific Reports*, vol. 6, no. 1, p. 32986, viewed 16 September 2021.

Seo, M-G & Barrett, LF 2007, 'Being Emotional during Decision Making: Good or Bad? An Empirical Investigation', *The Academy of Management Journal*, vol. 50, no. 4, pp. 923–40.

Chapter 17

Critcher, CR, Dunning, D & Armor, DA 2010, 'When Self-affirmations Reduce Defensiveness: Timing Is Key', *Personality and Social Psychology Bulletin*, vol. 36, no. 7, pp. 947–59.

Harber, KD, Yeung, D & Iacovelli, A 2011, 'Psychosocial resources, threat, and the perception of distance and height: Support for the resources and perception model', *Emotion*, vol. 11, no. 5, pp. 1080–90.

Sherman, DK 2013, 'Self-affirmation: Understanding the Effects', *Social and Personality Psychology Compass*, vol. 7, no. 11, pp. 834–45.

Chapter 18

Adams, S 2013, 'How to Build Willpower for the Weak', *Time*, viewed 12 December 2023.

Baumeister, RF 2014, 'Self-regulation, ego depletion, and inhibition', *Neuropsychologia*, vol. 65, pp. 313–19.

de Haan, T & van Veldhuizen, R 2015, 'Willpower depletion and framing effects', *Journal of Economic Behavior & Organization*, vol. 117, pp. 47–61.

Hoffer, A & Giddings, L 2015, 'Exercising Willpower: Differences in willpower depletion among athletes and nonathletes', *Contemporary Economic Policy*, vol. 34, no. 3, pp. 463–74.

Oettingen, G & Reininger, KM 2016, 'The power of prospection: mental contrasting and behavior change', *Social and Personality Psychology Compass*, vol. 10, no. 11, pp. 591–604.

Sander, L 2023, '"Disastrous experiment": Real reason behind hated return to work push', *news.com.au*, 8 June, viewed 12 December 2023.

Snoek, A, Levy, N & Kennett, J 2016, 'Strong-willed but not successful: The importance of strategies in recovery from addiction', *Addictive Behaviors Reports*, vol. 4, pp. 102–7.

Russ, S, Rout, S, Sevdalis, N et al. 2013, 'Do Safety Checklists Improve Teamwork and Communication in the Operating Room? A Systematic Review', *Annals of Surgery*, vol. 258, no. 6, pp. 856–71.

Key 5 intro

Topolinski, S & Reber, R 2010, 'Gaining Insight Into the "Aha" Experience', *Current Directions in Psychological Science*, vol. 19, no. 6, pp. 402–5.

Thrash, TM, Elliot, AJ, Maruskin, LA & Cassidy, SE 2010, 'Inspiration and the promotion of well-being: Tests of causality and mediation', *Journal of Personality and Social Psychology*, vol. 98, no. 3, pp. 488–506.

Chapter 21

Dompnier, B, Darnon, C & Butera, F 2009, 'Faking the Desire to Learn', *Psychological Science*, vol. 20, no. 8, pp. 939–43.

Elliot, AJ 1999, 'Approach and avoidance motivation and achievement goals', *Educational Psychologist*, vol. 34, no. 3, pp. 169–89.

Elliot, AJ & Thrash, TM 2002, 'Approach-avoidance motivation in personality: Approach and avoidance temperaments and goals', *Journal of Personality and Social Psychology*, vol. 82, no. 5, pp. 804–818.

Felix, A 2022, 'An Olympic Champion's Mindset for Overcoming Fear', TED talk, *YouTube*, viewed 28 September 2022.

Goswami, R 2022, 'Visualization: Allyson Felix Reveals This Training Mindset Helped Her Stay Competitive At 36 Years', *Essentially Sports*, viewed 12 December 2023.

Morris, RL & Kavussanu, M 2008, 'Antecedents of approach-avoidance goals in sport', *Journal of Sports Sciences*, vol. 26, no. 5, pp. 465–76.

Reiss, S 2012, 'Intrinsic and Extrinsic Motivation', *Teaching of Psychology*, vol. 39, no. 2, pp. 152–6.

Theis, D, Sauerwein, M & Fischer, N 2019, 'Perceived quality of instruction: The relationship among indicators of students' basic needs, mastery goals, and academic achievement', *British Journal of Educational Psychology*, vol. 90, no. 1, pp. 176–92.

Further reading

Introductory

Bedford, Louise, *Charting Secrets: Trade Like a Machine and Finally Beat the Markets Using These Bulletproof Strategies*, 2nd edition, May 2013.

Bedford, Louise, *Trading Secrets: Killer Trading Strategies to Beat the Markets and Finally Achieve the Success You Deserve*, 3rd edition, March 2012.

Bedford, Louise, *The Secret of Candlestick Charting: Strategies for Trading the Australian Markets*, February 2012.

Bedford, Louise, *The Secret of Candlestick Charting Poster and The Secret of Pattern Detection Poster*, available at www.tradinggame.com.au

Intermediate-advanced

Bedford, Louise, *Psychology MasterClass*, available via www.tradinggame.com.au/masterclass

Bedford, Louise, *The Secret of Writing Options: An Australian Guide to Trading Options for Profit,* February 2012.

Bedford, Louise, *Candlestick Charting Home Study Course* available via www.tradinggame.com.au

Acknowledgements

To **Chris Tate**, thank you for being my business partner and for all the adventures we've been on together over the years.

To **Scott Lowther**, my systems tester and friend. You are a sterling individual and I'm so grateful you've made this journey with me.

To **Germaine McCarthy**, my voice teacher. How can I ever thank you for enabling me to speak again? Your techniques and constant encouragement have meant more to me than you can know.

To **Allan Millett**, my physiotherapist. Your diligence and professionalism when I couldn't speak were above and beyond the call of duty. You have a gift!

And finally, to **Chris**, my husband, and to our children, **Ramona** and **Ash**. You are my foundation and strength.

Some of the concepts and topics explored throughout this book originally appeared as articles in my free monthly newsletter, available when you register on www.tradinggame.com.au, are explored on my www.talkingtrading.com.au podcast or covered in blog articles on my website. Check them out for yourself. Register on both websites so we can stay in touch.

Also by Louise Bedford

Charting Secrets, Revised Edition

Are you tired of letting the markets hit you in the hip pocket? Does following complicated strategies just not cut it anymore? Do you want your trading business to run on autopilot?

Well, you need to trade like a machine! Only then will you finally beat the markets and achieve the trading success you deserve. More workbook than technical reference, this user-friendly updated edition of Louise Bedford's best-selling book *Charting Secrets* will show you how easy and intuitive trend-spotting can be.

Become a self-assured trader who is capable of spotting hidden pockets of money in the markets. Take control of your own destiny and let Louise be your trading mentor.

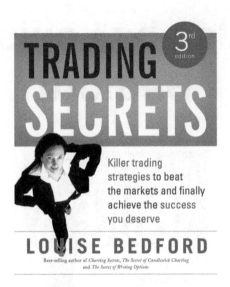

Killer trading strategies to beat the markets and finally achieve the success you deserve

LOUISE BEDFORD

Best-selling author of *Charting Secrets, The Secret of Candlestick Charting* and *The Secret of Writing Options*

Trading Secrets, 3rd Edition

Are you sick of watching your hard-earned funds slip away? Can you taste trading success but just don't know how to achieve it? Do you want to discover how to trade consistently and profitably?

Whether you're a novice trader or already in the game, this third edition of *Trading Secrets* is packed with everything you need to get in on the action. Known for her witty and entertaining style, Louise Bedford has demystified the world of share trading for thousands of investors and traders, and you're next!

Inside you'll find fascinating insights into: handling a windfall profit, identifying clear entry and exit signals, understanding the psychological factors that affect trading performance, setting stop losses and managing money.

Full of practical advice from an expert who has figured out the markets for herself, *Trading Secrets* is the book you need to get the most out of the world of trading.

The Secret of Candlestick Charting

Most traders in the Australian stock and futures markets begin by using conventional bar charts to generate buy and sell signals — until they discover the analytical power of candlestick charting.

This Japanese technique dates back over 300 years. Candlestick charts pinpoint trend changes prior to many other methods. Whether you are a beginner or a sophisticated investor, you can learn how to use candlestick charting to trade the markets profitably, beginning with your next trade.

In this book you will discover a technique that has the potential to completely alter the way you view charting, yet is complementary to any of the knowledge you have accumulated so far about technical analysis. Written in easy-to-understand language, these techniques are highly recommended for any traders or investors who wish to develop their technical analysis abilities and enhance their profitability.

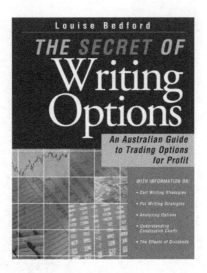

The Secret of Writing Options

Once thought to be the domain of highly skilled investors, today more and more private investors and traders are entering the options market. One of the big attractions of options trading is that, unlike a traditional investor, an options trader can still make money in a sideways-trending or falling market.

This book is highly recommended for newcomers to options trading in Australia, and those already trading in the options markets. It starts with the basics, and discusses the discipline and attitude necessary to trade successfully. There is also a cleverly constructed game to play to see if you are ready to enter the options market.

"Somewhere inside you there is a brilliant trader wanting to come out."

From the trading desk of Louise Bedford...

Louise Bedford
Your Trading Mentor

Louise Bedford here.

I'm on a quest!

A quest to create as many happy, independent, wealthy and skilled share traders as possible.

Make no mistake—successfully trading the sharemarket is one of the most valuable skills you'll ever learn. Once you know how to trade, **no-one can ever take this ability away from you**.

It's with you for life. The rewards will keep rolling in for you and your entire family.

Register now on my website and I'll give you my free five-part e-course and help you **finally nail the simple trading secrets necessary to make your profits soar**.

And just imagine, instead of battling on and struggling to work out the hidden secrets of the market all by yourself, you'll **feel secure and gain the confidence** that every exceptional trader needs to excel.

If you're serious about creating a better life for you and your family, then please don't wait with this one. You have absolutely nothing to lose by getting online right now.